LETTERS

FROM

Henry Miller

TO

Hoki Tokuda Miller

LETTERS

FROM

Henry Miller

TO

Hoki Tokuda Miller

Edited by Joyce Howard

FREUNDLICH BOOKS

New York

Copyright © 1986 by Hoki Tokuda Miller and Joyce Howard
Published by Freundlich Books
(A division of Lawrence Freundlich Publications, Inc.)
212 Fifth Avenue
New York, N.Y. 10010
Distributed to the trade by Kampmann & Company
9 East 40th Street
New York, N.Y. 10016
Manufactured in the United States of America
10 9 8 7 6 5 4 3 2 1

Library of Congress Cataloging-in-Publication Data
Miller, Henry, 1891–
Letters from Henry Miller to Hoki Tokuda Miller.
1. Miller, Henry, 1891–   —Correspondence.
2. Tokuda, Hoki—Correspondence. 3. Authors,
American—20th century—Correspondence. I. Tokuda,
Hoki. II. Howard, Joyce, 1922–   . III. Title.
PS3525.I5454Z496   1986   818 .5209   86–8874
ISBN 0–88919–038–4

Contents

Introduction

Henry Miller was in his late seventies when I met him through my friendship with Anaïs Nin. During visits to his home in the Pacific Palisades, I was always fascinated by the great variety of moods in which one would find him: sometimes full of vigor, buffoonery, and clowning around; another time positively truculent, when reading a review of a newly acclaimed book, which, he would growl, "It's far dirtier than anything *I* ever wrote!" (So it still hurt that the great novels he wrote in the thirties, *Tropic of Cancer*, *Tropic of Capricorn*, *Black Spring*, and so forth, were banned in his own country until the sixties. And this after immediate world-wide success in Europe and Japan!) Then, there was the sadness. Hoki Tokuda Miller, from whom he was then separated, would visit occasionally, and one could only wonder at her particular beauty. But when she left, I felt the keening in him.

Henry once described himself as "a confused, negligent, reckless, lusty, obscene, boisterous, thoughtful, scrupulous, lying, diabolically truthful man . . . filled with wisdom and nonsense." Certainly he was all of that, and Gurdjieff would have approved and understood so many "heads." But there was one more I never knew then and wish now that I had. It is revealed so poignantly and unexpectedly in the following correspondence.

Sometime after Henry's death, I received a phone call from Hoki, who reminded me of our occasional meetings. She asked if I would be interested in seeing and working with all the correspondence from Henry, who had given her permission to publish it after his death. I was intrigued—even more so when basket after Japanese basket was brought down my canyon stairs, containing hundreds of letters, cards, photos, and articles!

However, there were few letters or cards from Hoki, as she had difficulty writing English at that time. I was at a loss how to balance the book. Then I realized, if there was no response from her in this complex relationship in words, why not try *images*? Because her remarkable quality, then as now, is her gentle, unaffected humor and warmth. She only has to walk into a room and it's as though someone has turned up the thermostat. She's quite unaware of this effect on people, being a truly modest person. But I hope her photographs will show not only this essense but also her vulnerability, which Henry found so tantalizing.

Norman Mailer maintains that "Henry could not write about fucking with love." Well, he certainly does in these intimate and ultimately heartbreaking letters. Was it part of his "scrupulousness" that kept such deep and private emotions out of his literary work? Because surely the Henry who was unable to sleep at two or three o'clock in the morning, who was compelled to paint yet another haunted watercolor of Hoki's face, who poured out his yearning for her in letters (some of which he never even dared to send her)— surely this is another aspect altogether of the complicated man they called the "ram."

There is an interesting background to this extraordinary and obsessive love. As a boy, Henry Miller never experienced affection of any kind from his mother, as is manifest in a quote from *My Life and Times*:

> I never felt any warmth from her. She never kissed me, never hugged me. I don't ever remember going to her and putting my arms around her. I didn't know mothers did that till one day I visited a friend at his home. We were twelve years old. I went home from school with him and I heard his mother's greeting: "Jackie, oh Jackie," she says, "Oh darling, how are you, how have you been?" She puts her arms around him and kisses him. I never heard that kind of language—even that tone of voice. It was new to me. Of course, in that stupid German neighbourhood, they were great disciplinarians, really brutal people.

In the interim years Miller became attracted by the Orient—he read widely about China and Japan. In a letter to Anaïs Nin in

INTRODUCTION

October 1933, he tells her about seeing the film of "Madame Butterfly" and says, "Whether it's because I am becoming so definitely Oriental or what, I don't know, but I am stirred by it all over again." And in the same letter he gives her a list of books to read, including two on China and *Tales of Old Japan*. He also describes his austere room at Clichy in France, saying it has an Oriental character—full of harmony and philosophic calm. And in another letter to Nin in 1938, he tells her he's "a Chinaman at heart."

Who can tell how much this absorbing interest in the Orient may have prepared his unconscious mind for Emil White's letter from Japan, which Jay Martin describes in *Always Merry and Bright, the Life of Henry Miller*:

> His old friend Emil White . . . wrote from Japan that Miller should go to that country to find "one last wife." He had always been fascinated by the whole notion of the Geisha and dreamed of having a perfect Geisha for a wife—being loved without discrimination and, if need be, without desert. . . . The ideal image of the devoted Oriental woman shimmered in his mind.

So, Henry had come to believe more and more in the power of love. He wrote to Lawrence Durrell about Goethe, who, in his seventies had a love affair with a girl of nineteen and wrote an ecstatic poem about her. Henry also admired the success of Pablo Casal's marriage at eighty to a girl of twenty. And he wanted to fall romantically in love. All these longings seemed to fall softly into place when he got to know Hoki Tokuda. She was young, innocently beautiful, and a talented pianist and singer in many languages, who, with her mother, had studied music at the conservatory in Ontario, Canada. When Henry met her at the home of his physician and friend, Dr. Siegel, she had been in America only a few weeks and had started to perform at the Imperial Gardens. Yet she was independent, self-willed, and certainly no Geisha, as he would discover!

So, this East-West, April-October relationship began when Henry was seventy-five and Hoki was twenty-eight. It is a psychological jigsaw puzzle, and because of the extraordinary personalities involved, it is also a unique one.

At the end of their marriage, Henry wrote his book about Hoki, with paintings, called *Insomnia*, in which he says:

> To be sure, she never read all my letters, for the simple reason I didn't mail them all. Half of them are in my quaint old New England chest. Some of them are marked and stamped "Special Delivery." (What a touching thing it would be if some one sent her these after I am six feet under!) Then, to paraphrase my beloved idol I could whisper from above: "My dear Koi-bito [sweetheart], how sweet to read these *rabu reta* [love letters] over God's shoulder." As the French say—"*Parfois il se produit un miracle, mais loin des yeux de Dieu.*" God isn't interested in miracles. After all, life itself is just one prolonged miracle. It's when you're madly in love that you look for miracles.

And, of course, someone did give Hoki those "Special Delivery" letters. And with all the others, as he hoped, "over God's shoulder," here they are.

Joyce Howard
Santa Monica,
California

Part I

FALLING IN LOVE

In 1966, when Henry Miller was seventy-five, he was living in Pacific Palisades in California. His work had finally been published and acclaimed in America, after being banned for years. *Tropic of Cancer* was published in 1961; *Tropic of Capricorn, Black Spring, A Private Correspondence with Lawrence Durrell* in 1963, and the trilogy *The Rosy Crucifixion* and *Letters to Anaïs Nin* in 1965.

In February of 1966, Henry went to play ping-pong with his good friend and physician, Dr. Lee Siegel, where he met Hoki Tokuda. She was a beautiful Japanese woman of twenty-seven, recently arrived from her country. She was also an accomplished Jazz singer and pianist. Soon Henry started to haunt the Imperial Gardens where she performed, and he fell deeply and romantically in love with her.

The first three photographs he sent her were of the photograph of himself aged three.

/\/\/\/\/\/\/\

February 22, 1966

Dear Hoki

I hope to see you one evening this week at the Imperial Gardens. Maybe I will bring my friend Joe Gray along. He wants to meet nice Japanese girl.

Henry Miller

3

/\/\/\/\/\/\/\

March 23, 1966

Dear Hoki

Just a little word to let you know I am thinking of you. If you are free Saturday afternoon—about three o'clock—and want to play more ping pong, come to Frank Tashlin's house. My best to you always—and to your sister.

Henry *san*

/\/\/\/\/\/\/\

March 25, 1966

Dear Hoki san

Had another big night last night at the gallery. Am really tired now. Am thinking of you always and hope you find a house soon. If possible I will see you before Sunday but I am not sure. I have very much work to do now.

Henry X X X

/\/\/\/\/\/\/\

In April, he sent her five postcards of his own watercolors, with an ongoing message on them:

4

/∖.∨.∖∧.∖∧.∨.∖∧

ONE FISH

Dear Hoki—That silk handkerchief (Utamaro) was a very lovely gift. I appreciate it very much. (Arigato!) Do they have others with work by Hiroshiga and Hokusai? Where could I find them please? Get plenty of sleep! Maybe I will see you Saturday at Tashlin's for ping pong???

Henry Miller

/∖.∨.∖∧.∖∧.∨.∖∧

THE ANCESTOR

Same day (card 2) WU WEI

Some years ago I gambled at Monte Carlo, according to a system. It took too long to win—was like holding down a job! Dostoievsky, my favorite writer, was a compulsive gambler and always lost. He used to pawn his wife's petticoats in order to play. He was an epileptic.

(continued on next card)

/∖.∨.∖∧.∖∧.∨.∖∧

THE HAT AND THE MAN

It was an American who opened Japan to the world and an American (Babcock) who introduced Mah Jongg to U.S. from

China. Russ Tamblyn, actor friend of mine, just back from Japan, told me strange stories about your country today. Another friend, a Frenchman in diplomatic service told me that Pierre Loti was a homosexual,

(continued)

/\/\\/\\/\\/\\/\

DEUX JEUNES FILLES
Card 4 . . . and hated women. Mme Chrysanthème was probably a boy friend who treated him badly. How do you like that? Tonight I saw Prof. Ito, a Japanese wrestler, defeat an American boxer—at wrestling. Nice Judo chops! Honorable Ito-San very charming— beard and all. Sleep well now so that when

(continued)

/\/\\/\\/\\/\\/\

REALLY THE BLUES
Card 5 Friday comes you can do a Mah Jongg Marathon for 3 days and nights without stopping. I am now eating sashimi and black radish for lunch everyday. Gives me more backbone to defend myself against Honorable seductresses from Japan, China, Burma, Siam, Vietnam, Annam and so on. Soon I develop heart of cast iron.

Henry-San

FALLING IN LOVE

ᴧᴧᴧᴧᴧᴧ

Dear Hoki

Tonight you looked more beautiful than ever. Every time I look at you I wonder are you happy or sad. Always there is the mask. But sometimes I think I can see behind the mask—like Alice stepping through the mirror. I would love to fall in love with you, but I know that you are only in love with love. God bless you!

Your friend—
Henry San

ᴧᴧᴧᴧᴧᴧ

May, 1966

Dear Hoki

Watakushi no koi bito!*

Here is a little picture from Hiroshiga's "Tokaido." This must be the "steam bath" that Joe is always talking about. The writing on the back is by my Japanese friend Ueno-San of Ichinoseki City (Iwate Pref.)

When do I get the massage you promised me?

I have written to a music shop in Paris to send me the album (for you) of Jacqueline François "The Soul of a Poet."

I hope you won a lot of money last night. I also hope you had some sleep.

When you feel rested, not nervous, not impatient, not frustrated, sit down and write me a letter—and don't worry about mistakes in English. I would understand you even if you wrote in Swahili!

Your romantic friend

Henry-San

* My sweetheart, my lover!

/\.\/\.\/\.\/\.\

June 25, 1966
Night of the Stars

To Hoki

Tonight you are still more wonderful than ever. Tonight I lifted the mask a tiny wee bit—to catch a glimpse of your soul. All is brightness, softness, tenderness. It inspires me to write you a few lines in Japanese—like this:

Anawata kokosau i ju machi takeawa mori sansumatu okobichi imusato onosara bimono sai—meiji watasi obichneko kokoro.*

Fidelement votre

Sensei Homru

* watasi = my, kokoro = heart. The rest is Henry's Japanese Jabber-wocky! Ed.

FALLING IN LOVE

/\/\.\/\.\/\.\/\.\/\.\/\.\

6/29/66

Dear Hoki—Just a little word to tell you how very lovely you looked in your native garb last night.

I am still trying to find the record by Jacqueline François—"The Soul of a Poet"

I'll see you when you return from San Francisco

Be good. Take care of yourself *"repeatedly,"* as they say in Japanese.

Henry

/\/\.\/\.\/\.\/\.\/\.\/\.\

July 3rd 1966

Dear Hoki Horiko Kokoro-Ko!*

Good morning! Did you have a good trip to San Francisco? I missed you! I was going to call you up last night but—I fell asleep. (Forgive me!) Did you win a lot of money? I hope so.

Henry-San is thinking about you all the time—if you are happy, if you are nervous, if you are impatient, and so on.

Last night you looked lovelier than ever. Each time I tell you the same thing—but it's true.

It means that you are growing on me. Little by little you are wearing down all my defenses. Soon I will be helpless. Then you will be happy. A victory!

If only I could write you or talk to you in Japanese! What things we could tell each other!

Now I am sitting in a restaurant—Frascati's. I am having whipped cream in my coffee. The waitress is from Paris—Montmartre. We

9

talk about simple things in French. It makes me feel good. As if someone gave me a massage. My soul cools off. I become like a child again—*innocent*.

No room for more now. Too bad. I could write thousands of words just to tell Hoki-Ko what a wonderful woman she is. Now you must write me a few words. Yes?

Je t'embrace tendrement.

Henry-San

*My dear heart.

/\.\/\.\/\.\/\

7/12/66

Watakushi—no koi bito!*

My Japanese—I see that "pinto-ga awani".** Forgive me! I enclose a rather funny letter from an unknown fan. Notice the last paragraph! How goes it in your honorable house—"O-ouchi"?***

I may talk to you on the telephone before you receive this. My friend Mr. Gimpel (pianist) and his wife can't go to the Imperial Gardens this week. Next week, yes. I may come *this* Wednesday (tomorrow) for dinner, with Josette Hasson, the young lady from Egypt. If you are free, join us for dinner.

Now I must write a letter "watashi no musuko ni."****

I have a kimono, the geta, the obi, a fan, a parasol—but all this is not enough to make me a good Japanese. "Areba yo gozoimasu ga!"***** Maybe in my next incarnation I will become a real *Sensei*. And then I will play the samisan or the koto. Or write beautiful poems like Basho, or paint beautiful women, like Utamaro. Then I wouldn't mind if some beautiful Madame Chrysanthemum should break my heart. It has been broken so many times I don't worry about it anymore. Always willing to lose it to the right comer.

This doesn't make much sense, does it? It's just an excuse to say a few words to you.

Stay well, keep your throat clear, preserve your appetite and keep your heart open.

Je t'embrasse.

Henry-San

    * "My dear sweetheart."
    ** "I cannot focus (my Japanese)."
    *** "house."
    **** "I must write a letter to my son."
    ***** "If only I had more! (Japaneseness)"

/\/\/\/\/\/\
.•..•..•..•..•.

July 20, 1966

Dear Hoki—koi bito!*

I can't get the Ravel harp record till next week, so I give you in the meantime some Flamenco. Plus my Water Color Album which I promised you long ago.

Here is the article by Marianne Ruuth. Would you please return it to me Friday evening when I come again to dinner with Mr. and Mrs. Gimpel.

If it makes you nervous to have him sit at bar and watch you we could take a table alongside the bar. You tell us.

Cheers now!

    Bless you!

Henry-San

P.S. When do I get the "gokuraku—ojo"?

    * "my sweetheart."

11

/\.\/\.\/\.\/\.\

HELP BRING LOVE TO THE WORLD!
DON'T PLAY MAH JONGG!
PLAY THE KOTO LIKE A ROBOT!
(Advice to the lovelorn)
by
Prof. (Sensei) Valentino
Mira.

/\.\/\.\/\.\/\.\

7/17/66

Dear Hoki

In writing to Anaïs Nin today I couldn't resist sending you the letter she wrote me about her first impressions of your dear country. I am sure she is writing about it in her Diary—Vol. 183 or 192!! And you will live to read it one day, even if I will not.

In page one of your letter I was struck by a phrase you used— "l feel that I have recovered my heart" (listening to Ravel). This is beautiful. No English writer would have said it just this way. It is correct but most unusual. Yours is better than anything "we" might say.

This heart (kokoro) is very much with me each time I see you. I want you to know it is my heart you have reached. I believe in the heart—it is always right, even when it leads to sadness or despair. ("The Wisdom of the Heart" is the title of one of my books.)

Lately, and because of you, I believe my interest in good music has come back strong. (I am now listening to Bach's "Mass in B minor" Stupendous!)

FALLING IN LOVE

Must stop now—going to the Siegels for ping pong. Maybe I will see you there. If not enjoy the bull fight! Olé! Olé!

Your

Cocorico!

Henry-San

/\/\\./\\.\/\\.\/\\.\/\\.\/\\./\

July 20, 1966
(Midnight)

(Just home from Imperial Gardens)

Hoki darling—

Every time I see you I get a little happier—and a little sadder too. Happy because I see you once again, sad because I see you for only a little while. What to do about it? I don't know. We are moving on different levels. We are like trains that pass each other in the night. Hello! Goodbye! Till next time. Sayonara! A bientôt! My eyes are still looking into yours and drowning there; I see your hair waving and I wander alone in a bamboo forest, bewitched by your smile which comes and goes like clouds racing through a summer's sky. I feel so close to you and yet I am a thousand light years away. I thank you for making my heart beat again—if only it would burst! The days fly, and I remain, love growing stronger all the time. Ah yes, "love *is* a many splendored thing!" You make me rich.

Blessings on you, my beloved Hoki! Speak to me in your dreams —I am listening.

My ears are still filled with the sound of your voice;

Henry-San

13

/.Λ.Λ.Λ.Λ.Λ.\

7/26/66

Hoki-San—

How are you? Good morning—or is it Good Evening? Take good care of yourself—*repeatedly*. Don't gamble your life away! Or, if you do, save me your heart (kokoro), please. I will wear it on my sleeve.

Henry-San

/.Λ.Λ.Λ.Λ.Λ.\

August, 1966
Sunday midnight
(Day of the blue peacock)

Dear, dear Hoki—

It was such a good day. I am still drunk with happiness. Strange, because when we got back to your house I was on the point of saying I will never see you again. I couldn't possibly live with you if you were like the woman you pretended to be in the restaurant. But you are not that sort of person—and you made it clear to me. And I believe you. But I think maybe you are a little uncertain, a little confused, perhaps even afraid of facing reality. We have had so little time together, so few intimate talks, so little chance to come to grips with one another. Right or wrong, I have the impression that you were playing a game with me—and it hurt me, hurt my pride. Why should we play games? You are a woman, not a teen-ager. I expect you to be honest and frank with me.

You are the only one I truly love, and I love you with all my heart. I know many women, I see many women, but it means noth-

14

ing. I see them out of desperation—because I can't see you, be with you, love you as I want to. (I know the same is for you. I get jealous when I sit at the piano bar and see all the men who look at you so hungrily.) At the same time, in spite of our ability to attract the other sex, I feel there is a strong bond between us. I feel we belong to one another, that we could make one another happy. More than that—I feel we could help one another to lead a richer, fuller life. But to do this we have to see more of one another, share our thoughts and feelings, find out if we really are suited for one another or if it is only a dream, an illusion.

I was overjoyed when you said you would look for another place. This would give me the opportunity, I thought, to be closer to you, see you more often, more intimately. How can I know what you really feel about me until we establish a more intimate relationship? What have we to lose by knowing one another better? I could marry you tomorrow to help you get your visa, but that would not be a real marriage. If I marry you it will be because you love me, you want me, you won't be happy without me. If I am to have you, I want all of you, body and soul. I don't mean that I want to possess you. I want you to have your freedom, as an individual, but I would like to believe that you could find this freedom through loving me. I believe I have much to give you, just as you have much to give me. Even if you don't read my books you must know that I have had a life rich in experiences, all kinds of experience. And if I sometimes behave as a little boy, or a clown, I hope you know that I am also a man of the world, an adventurer, an artist, and some times almost a saint, almost a "Sensei". I know who I am and what I am, very definitely. I can still learn, still make mistakes, still do foolish things. I live completely in the present, and with one foot in the grave. Life has been good to me—or perhaps I should say that God has. I am living on grace, living beyond my time. And this makes me appreciate life more, makes me love more, makes me hungry for still more wonderful experiences.

Because of the great differences in our age I have acted rather shy with you. It has taken me a long time to expect of you anything like the admission of love I make to you. From that night that Joe

15

and I took your sister and you home to your old place—when you sat in my lap and stroked my hand, remember? I felt that there was something between us. And then things cooled off, it seemed to me. Whenever I wanted to be with you, spend real time with you, you always had excuses—horse races, Tijuana, guests, Mah Jongg, and so on. Henry-San was always willing and ready to give up anything to see Hoki-San, if only for an hour or so at dinner. But Hoki-San —she seemed to belong to the world. She was not "romantic". She was self-sufficient, needed nobody, nothing. She had no lover, she said. Which made everything more mysterious. Was this how a Japanese woman was, I asked myself? Has she no feelings? Is she just a beautiful doll who smiles at all men alike? Is she just an entertainer—a sing-song girl—for whom the public is everything?

And so we come to Mika-San. It is true enough that I find her interesting and attractive—certainly more so than any of the other waitresses—but the real reason I wanted to date her was to see if Hoki-San was indifferent or not. I am sure that if I were to go out with her all I would be thinking of the whole evening would be ——— *Hoki*. (But you would probably not believe that.)

Another thing you probably won't believe is that I have had three proposals of marriage in the last six weeks. (In addition there are two women in New York begging me to come and live with them) one in Paris, one in Berlin, and one in Warsaw, Poland. And I'm not joking. I don't tell you these things to prove that I am the great lover, the irresistible Don Juan, but simply to let you know that I am not entirely out of the race, so to speak. And what you never will believe is that I confess to these women that I am helplessly in love with a beautiful Japanese girl, meaning none other than Her Imperial Highness, Hoki-Sama.

Now what does my dear Hoki have to tell me? It was such a good, happy day for me. (Only a little twinge of jealousy because Duke was there and perhaps also in love with Hoki-San.) You made me feel that you were truly happy to see me. I felt sure of it. I came straight home and sat down immediately to write you. The romantic

16

idiot? What matter! I can't wait till I see you again. I love you, love you, love you. Please don't ever say to me again—"I'll think about it." No games. Yes or no. Speak from your heart.

Let me add in closing that Nola likes you very much. She hoped that you would make me happy. And I think I made her happy by fixing it for her with my astrologer friend . . . It's after one o'clock. I'm tired. And you are probably wide awake at the Mah Jongg table. Let's hope the poker games are not going to take up all your spare time.

Your devoted

Henry-San
(enjoying his "Japanese sickness")

/\/\.\/\.\/\.\/\.\

Thursday noon

Dear Hoki-Sama—

Came home real drunk this morning. You will have to take better care of me! Anyway, here's the first message to your new home (my hands are still trembling).

Tomorrow, Friday, I'm coming to the gardens for dinner with the Chinese Actress Lisa Lu and her agent Bessie Loo (also Chinese). They are taking me to the Coconut Grove later in the evening. I hope we can come down to the bar for a little while. If you like stop by at our table for dessert.

If Jennifer Jones gets back from Vietnam next week I will bring her to meet you.

Even Ava Gardner is a little jealous of you!

Get sleep now—don't let the Chin-chin* Kobakama keep you awake! (To make sure, always destroy your tooth-pick after using it!)

17

Now I know *why* Chin-chin means what it does—in slang. Very poetic meaning originally! That's why we use the word "swinger," I guess.

Henry-San

* Penis.

ΛΛΛΛΛΛ

8/24/66

Dear, dear Hoki—

How good to see you again tonight. Strange evening. You were lovelier than ever. My two women friends adore you.

Don't let us forget to eat at L'Auberge on Sunset Blvd—near Curson. Good food. (French) One of those weekends when you don't play Mah Jongg till all hours of the morning, I want you to come here in the afternoon, have a swim, go to dinner with me and spend the whole evening with me. You owe me such an evening! And if you really love me you will do it. I love you more and more each time I see you.

Don't worry if I come to the bar with other women. I don't like to come alone. I am bringing them to see you, like I might bring you flowers. They all know I am madly in love with you.

Oh yes, I spoke to Mrs. Mori on the phone. Your painting should be ready this Saturday. I am eager to see how Mori-San framed it. I wish I could frame you, in flesh and blood, and hang you on my wall!

Good-night now. Lots of love and kisses. By the 29th of this month you will be having your pains gain.

Take care. Get good rest!

Henry-San

FALLING IN LOVE

∧.∨.∧.∨.∧.∨.∧

August, 1966

To the one and only

And still the Song of Love continues . . . Did you ever hear of the "curette"? It's the name of a surgical instrument with which they scrape the womb after an abortion. This afternoon it was as if you had used the curette on my soul. Now I can be sure that I will not die of "the Japanese sickness". Already I feel that the wound which was causing me pain and suffering is healing. I will live to fight another battle, maybe to fall in love even more violently than ever. What a surgeon you are! What a magician! And all without a drop of blood lost. I must note the day and the hour in my Book of Romantic Mishaps.

Really, my dear Hoki, you are stronger, more courageous, more honest, more tender too, than I had given you credit for being. I know that your frankness was prompted by a desire to protect me, protect me from any illusions which my crazy love sickness may have created. Which reminds me of a sentence from "The Tale of the Genji"—"It is usually the unexplored that attracts us, and Genji tended to fall most deeply in love with those who gave him the least encouragement."

I said that I had to accept you for what you are, not what I imagined you to be. Listening to you dissect yourself, reveal your faults, your failings, your weaknesses, was like participating in a drama in which the woman finally confesses to the lover she has been holding at a distance—"Very well, I give in; you may have me, but I want you to know I'm a leper." Cruel as such a situation may be, it's better than hearing her say—"The kind of love I want no man can give me."

If I gave you a sleepless night, and myself as well, it was because

19

it was one of the very rare times in my life, that I had to sleep beside a beautiful woman without touching her. When dawn came I was at least able to gaze at your countenance. What a world to study, to explore, in your night face! An entirely different face than Hoki wears in her waking moments. The face of a stranger, carved out of lava, like some oceanic goddess. More mysterious with eyes closed and features sculpted out of ancestral memories. An almost barbaric look, as if you had been resurrected from some ancient city—like Ankor Wat—or the submerged ruins of Atlantis. You were ageless, lost not in sleep but in the myth of time. I shall always remember this face of sleep long after I get to know the hundred and one faces you present to the world. It will be the dream face which you yourself have never seen and which I will guard as the sacred link between the ever-changing Hoki and the ever-searching Henry-San. This is my treasure and my solace.

It seems inevitable now that, being what I am, I shall one day write about you—whether in sorrow and despair or in joy and gratitude. With a few strokes of the pen I will erase forever the image of Madame Chrysantheme. *My* Kikou-San will be carved in jade, a jade long buried beneath the depths of the ocean. I would like it to be my swan song, a last burst of melody from the very heart of the passionate devotee of love. The *"Liebestraum"* sinking with the singer as he settles to the ocean's floor in peace and resignation.

I am glad you told me that, however difficult it may be for you to say "I love you," "I miss you," "I want you," "I need you," still I am always there (whenever, however, *there* maybe!) To be the "comforter" is no mean role. To know this is the best answer you could make to all my foolish questions and recriminations. It's like the Great Mother putting her finger to the lips of a child and saying —"Hush, baby, hush!"

I must stop now. It is eleven o'clock and I have had a wee bite to eat and two hours of marvelous conversation with some "psychodelic" youngsters who are off to tour the world.

20

FALLING IN LOVE

I will meet you tonight in my dreams. You will recognize me by
my laugh. And *you* will be singing the "Azumaya" which goes like
this: "The door is not bolted or barred. Come quickly and talk to
me. Am I another's bride, that you should be so careful and shy?"

Your Henry-San
saying "Good night!"

/\/\/\/\/\/\

Monday the Twelfth
(Day of the carrier Pigeon)

Dear Hoki,

When I came home yesterday I found the enclosed poster and
announcements from Shincho-sha. Is this the poster about "pornographic books" that I spoke to you about or is it one of my books?
I can't make it out. It seems to come from the editorial department
of their magazine, which is what puzzles me. Could it be, perhaps, an
announcement about Marianne Ruuth's article?

Ueno-San of Ichinoseki sent me a magazine, much like the one
Shincho-sha publishes, called (The Bungei Shunju." He had wanted
me to send my article on love ("Love and how it gets that way"
which appeared in "Mademoiselle" about three years ago) to this
magazine, but I told him I thought Shincho-sha's magazine was
better. Am I right? I am eager to see this text of mine translated
into Japanese, primarily so that *you* can read it. I know you don't
like to bother reading things in English.

I also enclose a letter from Mrs. Edith Fink, the friend who will
make the ring for you. If I get the stones (jades) in time I will
bring them with me tomorrow when I come to the Imperial Gardens
with my friends to eat. If you would still like your peacock stone

made into a ring, bring it with you and I will ask her to make it as well as the other. She talks, as you see, of using sterling silver. Would that be O.K. for both rings?

The other letter enclosed, from the editor of Yomiuri Shimbun, I send because of the "Quaint" English. Many letters from Japanese publishers and editors are in poor English. I often wonder why they can't hire secretaries who really know English? Anaïs Nin told me often that she met Japanese who pretended to know English, but she couldn't understand what they were saying to her. I had to laugh at the last sentence by Mr. Hirayam—"I will be your good guide of Tokyo night." Hurrah! Banzai!

Reading that I decided to send you the leaflet called "A Dream of a Book", which is all about a very unusual book I made with my brother-in-law from Jerusalem; it is called "into the Night Life". It sells for $250.00 a copy. One day, when your English has improved, I will give you a copy. Anyway, after my "night face" letter comes my "night guide" and my "Night Life" book. The night of nights!

I am going a little mad with all the work that has accumulated. It is only one o'clock in the afternoon and I have already done a full days work. I am going at it like a race horse. Will lose another three or four pounds at this rate. I can still see you standing on the scales, with dark glasses on, and a most curious expression on your face, as if to say—"Well, I'm holding my own—no lighter no heavier today, thank God!" And then you go off turned towards me, waved your little fingers like to say "Ciao!" (Italian) and slowly sauntered to the other room, dreamy but not unhappy (despite a restless night). Very Oriental, I thought. Loved it. Inside my little head there is a camera which constantly registers all your moods, all your expressions. My secret album!

I expect to get to the Imperial Gardens about 7.30 or 7.45 for dinner. If you are free, please join us. If not, I will see you at the piano bar. Have a good day today!

Henry-San

FALLING IN LOVE

/\.∧.∧.∧.∧.∧\

Dear Hoki—Anata bakari!*

This morning I learned over the telephone that my last wife (Eve) had just died in her sleep after a wonderful happy day. She was the best of all my wives (and mistresses), she did everything for me, and continued to do so even after we were divorced and she remarried. And I repaid her for all her goodness by running off to Europe with a worthless young bitch whom I grew tired of in a very short time.

At noon today I was weeping and sobbing fit to break my heart. I thought it would never stop. When it did I went to the Siegels to play ping pong—and then began an afternoon and evening during which I was as gay and alive as I have ever been. I ended up in a restaurant with four Canadian girls at my table and one on my lap. Still merry, more alive than ever, and finally dating the French waitress who happened to be one of my fans.

A few moments ago I woke up, sat like a statue, immovable—like a stone Buddha, but minus the seraphic smile—In those fifteen or twenty minutes of trance I reviewed my whole life with women. And I came to the conclusion that I am, and never was, any good for any woman.

I tell you this so that you know what I am and that you may rest easy in your soul. I shall never try to possess you, never expect anything of you, and warn you that even as a friend I may be no good.

If I love you it's because I can't help myself. Now I feel I can kill this love—because I know it's a selfish love. I had deluded myself into thinking that my love, whether returned or not, would exalt you.

I did *not*, as you seem to believe, give you gifts in order to bribe you. I gave them because I wanted to share with some one the joy which music has brought me. I have never tried to buy love.

23

You are a free woman and I hope you remain so. Save your love for Mah Jongg, horses, good food and the little things which cause no pain, no worry, no anxiety, no surrender of yourself. Be the sing-song girl which you are and stay with it.

Forget that you ever gave me a thought. Stay cool as a cucumber and pretend that you are happy, successful and adored by every one. You have nothing to lose but your soul.

I may be seeing you soon again but with another eye. Life is too short to waste it in search of the impossible. I have come to realize at last that what I thought was mystery hidden in the depths of your enchanting dark eyes is nothing more than a vacuum.

Your
Henry-San

* "My only one."

ΛΛΛΛΛΛ

9/20/66

Dear Hoki-San

Another interesting, perhaps extraordinary letter from my young Vietnamese friend—which I'd like back, of course.

Since writing this letter he wired me from Paris asking for $350.00 to go to Greece (and from there to India, where he will enter a monastery.) About ten days later I get a special delivery from Rome saying "Some bitch (a whore probably) had stolen all his money"—so I sent him more money. It pleases me to think that even a Zen monk, which he is, can become the victim of a greedy whore. He is quite a character obviously.

That's all.

Your Henry

FALLING IN LOVE

∧.∨.∧∧∧.∨.∧

9/25/66
(Hour of the horse—
month Naga Zuki) *

Dear Hoki—

Forgive me for thrusting the enclosed letter on you—I know that the handwriting is not easy to read. But I am so excited by this letter, I must share it with someone—and who better than you?

It is from my friend, who spent the last 25 years of his life in prison. (Remember me talking to you about him?) After ten or twelve years of struggle with the authorities, after spending a few thousand dollars for a worthless lawyer, after three visits to the Penitentiary (in Missouri) and *hundreds* of letters to my friend . . . . . . well, finally he was released on parole and sent to Chicago where he had committed most of his crimes. I tried to have him sent to me so that I could help him get on his feet, see that he did not drink (he was an alcoholic too) and find him a job, but they wouldn't permit that. However, in Chicago, where he has found a job already as a barber, he will be looked after by a great lawyer—a friend of mine, a Mr. Gertz, who also won my case with the Supreme Court (so that my books can be published now freely in America.)

I am trembling. I never quite believed the day would come when this man would walk out of prison. (He had been sentenced to life imprisonment, *plus* 28 years!!! Think of it!) It is as if I myself had been freed. What a victory! Anyway, save the letter and give it to me when I see you again, please.

My daughter (Val) informed me yesterday that she and her husband are divorcing as soon as possible, and then she will go somewhere to live by herself. Now I must definitely find a student, if possible, to come and live here, do the housework, cook me meals in the evening, and so on. If I can find a Japanese girl—and maybe Nobuko knows of one at U.C.L.A.—then I will take Japanese lessons, so that when I go to Japan next spring I will be able to speak a bit.

(The other night my cab driver told me he was born in Japan, lived there most of his life, and speaks it (Tokyo language) like a native. His father is a professor in a University, and though he is a scholar, does not speak as good Japanese as his son. (They are American, you understand.) I am going to have dinner with him at Imperial Gardens soon. Maybe interesting. He's not an ordinary cab driver!

Enclose leaflet sent me by Ueno-San after asking him about the Samurai film we saw.

The Siegels now have a young Japanese boy (a graduate of law school in Japan) with whom I had quite a talk yesterday. He is also a champion ping pong player, no one can stand up against him.

Oh yes, I gave the stones and ring to my friend, Mrs. Edie Fink, yesterday. It will take almost 2 weeks to do, because of other jobs she has. She showed me some of her best work—just wonderful! She's a true craftsman. Maybe I will ask her (later) to have dinner with us at Gardens and bring her show pieces along to show you what she can do. Your friends might like to buy interesting hand-made things for Xmas.

Please tell the woman in the shop at Imperial Gardens to be sure to save for me the "sake" set she showed me. I want to give it to Edie Fink** who is now interested in cooking Japanese style—has a Japanese cookbook and bought special pots and pans to cook Japanese dishes.

Oof! Never meant to write so much.

Your
Henry
(San not correct in signing
letters—remember?)

P.S. I was thinking to take a 2–3 weeks vacation in Haiti (West Indies) but now I'm not so sure. Have to see what my daughter does about divorce—may get a quick one in Mexico, or possibly an annulment.

* Month of September.
** I am, of course, going to pay Edie handsomely for the work she will do for you—the "sake" set is just a little token gift.

FALLING IN LOVE

/\.\/\.\/\.\/\.\

September, 1966

Dear Hoki—

Why don't you call me up tomorrow? I miss you. I am getting so tired of asking you to do this or that. Now I leave it to you—if you want to see me, eat with me, or whatever, *you* call *me*! I may go to Europe after all—for two or three weeks, on October 12th. There will be a special performance of the opera based on my book (The Smile at the Foot of the Ladder) in Hamburg, Germany. I want to be here to meet the Japanese actor—first week in October. I also must find someone to take care of my home before I go anywhere.

I am very tired—no real sleep for several weeks . . . You look so beautiful, it drives me crazy. Say something to me—don't let me feel I am talking and writing to a stone wall.

H.M.

/\.\/\.\/\.\/\.\

GIRL WITH BIRD

11/2/66 Dear Hoki-San Here's another card to add to your collection. it's an old painting I made for Val when she was a small child. Did you like the water color George brought you? If not, save it for me and I'll give you another. I can take out those "chin-chins" at bottom left if you wish.

What about the date, etc. of Japanese magazine?

Henry's present to Hoki, where, at her request, the "chin-chins" (Penises) at the bottom left of painting were covered by postage stamps!

27

/\.\/\.\/\.\/\.\/\.\/\.\

Oct. 1st 1966

Dear Hoki—

Here is the card for the framer who did the post cards of my water colors. I gave you a letter to him three or four weeks ago, telling him to frame your cards and let me pay for it. I guess you never read my letter!!

If you are free Monday evening maybe we could have dinner together and afterwards go to the McKenzie Art Gallery on La Cienega to see some supposedly spectacular paintings by a painter who lived in Tahiti. I will go, even if you don't wish to go. It sounds exciting to me.

Next Sunday, October 9th, my friend Gimpel, the pianist, is playing with a Symphony Orchestra at Royce Hall, U.C.L.A. 8oc P.M. I have tickets and will go—but I assume you would not be interested. If you are, you can let me know and I will give you a ticket.

Hope you don't have too much pain—cramps—these next few days.

Oh yes, will you bring the letters I asked for—from the Vietnamese boy and my convict friend, Roger B.

Hope to see you soon at Imperial Gardens.

Henry

/\.\/\.\/\.\/\.\/\.\/\.\

Thursday—10/20/66

Dear Hoki—

Would you do me a favor, please. Tell me the name of the enclosed magazine, the publisher, the date, and the name of the writer who has written the article about me. Then, if it is possible, ask one of my "fans" who visit the piano bar, if he would give me a rough translation of this text. I have an idea it may be very interesting. The reproductions of my paintings, especially those in color seem very well done. I also enclose the name of the person who sent me the magazine. Maybe *he* wrote the text. Do you recognize the name?

I am giving this to some one to deliver to you at the Gardens. I was hoping to come for dinner this evening but have been in bed all day with aches and pains (probably caught cold in the pool yesterday.)

Anyway, I hope to see you before I go. You can give me what information I asked for above then. And let me have the magazine back, if you don't find anyone to make a rough translation for me.

I forgot to write and thank the Japanese translator who sent me Tonoyama's book. Would you mind dropping him a card for me and say that I left for Hong Kong.

Now that I've changed the date of departure three times I'm beginning to wonder if I really am going to Hong Kong. More and more I feel like not going—maybe because I'm so very weary and sick at heart. But since I've committed myself I guess I will go through with it. I know in advance that I'm going to miss you, that no matter how many beautiful women will be put in my path I will be thinking only of you.

I had a wonderful letter yesterday from my astrologer-friend in Switzerland, telling me what is in store for me this coming year. And most of it was very, very good. But she said nothing about *voyages*, which she usually does. And that mystifies me. But what mystifies me most is *you*. Well, maybe I'll see everything more clearly when I get to Hong Kong. Maybe I'll see with new eyes.

Déwa mata!

Henry

/\.\/\.\/\.\/\.\

Dear Hoki-San—

I took the liberty of marking passages in this little book—I hope you won't take offense! Despite the fact that it is a *general* picture—for *all* Scorpios—there is much in it which I think fits you that I think it worth reading. Too bad you don't know, even approximately, the *time* you were born. It would help a lot.

Strangely enough, many of the *good* traits of Scorpio, I already recognized in you. The bad ones which we all have, I prefer not to think about. There is no question in my mind that you are a real Scorpio. And you know better than I what fits you in this general picture.

Anyway, I wish the best for you always. People who have difficult horoscopes are always the most interesting, even if they are hard to live with. If you can live with yourself, that is the big thing.

In "eternal friendship"

Your
Henry-San

P.S. I hope your agent won't be at your birthday party. I have come to detest this individual—even his looks.

/\.\/\.\/\.\/\.\

11/14/66

Dear Hoki—

I woke up too late this morning to mail the enclosed letter—birthday greetings—special delivery. And, not knowing for sure if you are still at Kirkwood Drive, I am sending this to the Imperial Gardens. I may be there Tuesday or Wednesday evening.

30

FALLING IN LOVE

Meanwhile in this morning's mail I received a clipping from "Josei Jishin" Tokyo. I have another copy and will try to find some-one to translate it for me, as I know you won't have time for it. I'm dying to know *who* wrote it and what it says. The photos were from the Westwood Art Exhibit, I notice. Except the one of you at right bottom page. Now *who* could have supplied that, I wonder? How long ago was this photo taken? Strange, but you look older in this photo than now!

I'm so angry with myself for not getting up in time that I'm going back to bed to dream it off.

Henry-San

/\/\/\/\/\/\

11/14/66
(2 A.M.)

Hoki-Sama:

The day has come. Congratulations! As an artist you belong with the stars above; as a woman with the flowers of the field; as a friend with the fiery gems buried in the bowels of the earth. Soon it will be time to assume your rightful role as Queen of Hearts!

Keep sipping the honey from every chalice that is proffered. The world is your oyster, if you wish it that way. Walk in beauty like the night, but make sure your path is strewn with rose petals. Stay cool as jade but never green with envy.

Adventure becomes you, so long as you keep Kwannon at your side.

Step blithely now into your thirtieth year. It is one you will never forget because your dear Sensei will be observing your every move, listening to your every thought, anticipating your wildest desires, invading your day and night dreams, and, unknown to you, shaping your brilliant future.

31

At ninety, God willing, he will still be your friend, still believe in you, still sing your praises.

If only he could say it all in Japanese you would take wing like a bird and never again know sorrow.

Henry-San
(From his solitary perch in Pacific Palisades)

/\.\/\.\/\.\/\.\/\.\

11/22/66

Dear Hoki-Sama—

This morning I received a letter from my astrologer friend in Switzerland, telling me much more, about you and me, our relationship in the heavens. I want to keep this wonderful information to myself for a while.

She begged me to get you to find out the *hour* of your birth, it is most important. Then she can give a full picture of your chart. Dear Hoki, could you not write to your mother and ask her to try to remember? If you were born in a hospital there may be a record of your birth *and the hour* there. If your mother can't recall the exact time, could she at least tell you if it was night or day? (I have a strong hunch that you were born sometime between two and five o'clock in the morning, because at that time you seem to be at your best.)

Sometimes a little detail will help a person to remember. The ringing of church bells, for example, the first rays of dawn, or when the first labor pains began—after dark, or when? You were born on a Sunday, it seems. Even in Japan Sunday is different from other days in the week, and so there could have happened things that day which would have helped her to remember.

So, once again, do please try. It may be of great value to you to know exactly what your chart tells about you. We have the general picture already, we know where the major planets are, but sometimes a difference of a few minutes can make a big difference in the interpretation of the chart.

I never saw you before as you were last night. When you started to dance I fell in love with you all over again. The Hoki I always wanted to know suddenly came to life.

I'm here
I expect to be at Imperial Gardens Wednesday at 8oc for dinner, with Sydney Omarr and two others. See you at the bar if not at dinner.

Your
Henry-San

/\/\.\/\.\/\.\/\.\/\

Thursday midnight

Good morning, dear night owl, and how is your butterfly to-day? I thought I would let you put this in the waste basket for me, along with your unwritten thoughts. This is a sheet of paper on which I tested my colors. I didn't have the heart to throw it away myself. Maybe you have a little private cemetery in which to bury spots of color, old love letters, broken feathers and other such trifles. If not, I will make one for you. Call at any hour of the day or night— always at your service. We also repair broken skulls and revive old skeletons.

Remember, the left hand is the dreamer—All dreams must be played in the key of C sharp minor!

Henry Valentine Miller
11/24/66

/\\.\\/\\.\\/\\.\\/\\.\\/\\.\\/\\.\\

My dear, dear Hoki—

I hope I have the courage to mail this letter and not put it away in a drawer, as I have with others I wrote you. For with this goes the last ounce of pride I possess. I have to know, I *must* know, whether you really love me or not. I have been in absolute torture for months now. I can't hold out much longer. I am truly at the end of my rope. I can't work, I can't sleep; my mind is on you perpetually, without let up. It's not a sickness any more, it's a mania. I am obsessed and possessed.

If you don't love me it would be a kindness if you told me so. As it is, I am left in the dark. I don't know what you think. It's like a cat and mouse game. It's not only painful to endure but it's ridiculous and, if you are doing it deliberately, it's unworthy of you. Do I deserve such treatment? Have I ever wounded you in any way?

I know one thing about you for certain, and that is that it is very difficult for you to reveal your true feelings. Why it should be God alone knows. Maybe at some time in your life you were badly hurt. Maybe you are simply trying to protect yourself. But why make *me* suffer, I whom you regard as a friend, a friend forever.

Do you realize that you give me less consideration, less attention than you would a lap dog? You told me once that you would rather be my girl friend than marry me. But you haven't even been *that*! I must tell you here that I did not know until very recently that when a man (according to Japanese custom) tells a woman he loves her it is equivalent to a proposal of marriage. I can understand now that you must have thought it strange that I did not make you a formal proposal. It may have hurt your pride too. Being a Westerner, I have always thought of love and marriage as two distinct things. I never thought it a dishonor to love a woman without marrying her. In fact, I even think that because I married I lost the love which led up to it . . . And then, do you not remember how one day, sitting in your kitchen, you told me you didn't like the idea of marriage, that you were afraid you would be bored, afraid you would lose your freedom, afraid you would have to have children, and so on and so on? I believed you then. I was willing to have you on your own terms. I thought possibly you told me all this so as not to deceive me, or hurt me. I did *not* believe all the bad things you ascribed to your character. I did *not* believe that if we were to live together, whether married or unmarried, you would make my life miserable. I had faith in love, not in you, not in me, but in the power of love to create beauty and harmony. At my age this must indeed sound naive—romantic, if you like—But I know of no greater power than love, do you?

Some people, including your own friends, have told me that I made a great mistake in letting you know how much I love you. They spoke as if I had become your "victim" through showing my hand so plainly. I know what they mean, these people. I am no fool. If I thought for one moment that that was your game I would despise you. I can be a willing slave, yes. It would give me pleasure to serve you, make you happy, help you live your own life. But I could never be dangled from a string like a puppet.

And now I want to bring you back to a telephone conversation we had some months ago. I was telling you very seriously that I was in love with you, that I loved you. And what did you say? "Then we must do something about it!" And there was a thrill in your voice as you said these words.

And what has happened since? I'll let you answer that for yourself.

Then came the interview in the Japanese magazine. I now know every line of it by heart. I thought, when I sent it to you to read, that perhaps you would translate it for me. But no, all you could tell me was that it was a very nice article, nothing to worry about. The things I would have given so much to hear from your own lips you kept to yourself. Didn't you ever think that I would find a way to get it translated, word for word?

It reminds me of the photo which you inscribed for me. When I asked you what you had written you turned your back and left the room. Why? Were you ashamed of what you had written? Can you possibly be so ungenerous as to refuse me even that little crumb of pleasure?

Today my heart jumped for joy when Sydney Omarr telephoned me that he had bumped into you strolling along Hollywood Boulevard at one in the afternoon, looking better than you ever did, and smiling as if all was well with the world. I could hardly believe my Hoki was up that early and taking a breath of fresh air. Oh, at last she is getting some sense, I thought—perhaps she will give me a ring, perhaps she will ask if we could dine together tonight. But no, no telephone, no dinner together. Just the usual "static".

People who know I love you are writing me, from all over the world, saying—"Give my love to Hoki. She must be a wonderful girl to make you lose yourself so completely".

You *are* a wonderful girl, a difficult girl, and sometimes you behave like a heartless girl. Which is the real Hoki? The one I believe in or the one you pretend to be?

Now that I am living alone here I am like a prisoner who paces back and forth in his cell, who scribbles crazy thoughts on the walls, who looks in vain for the sun and moon, who counts the days, the hours till his release. I am even worse off than that poor prisoner, because I have created my own prison, because I can torture myself in a thousand different ways, because I have too great an imagination, too much sensitivity, and because my mind is fixed not on release but on Hoki.

God alone can help me in my anguish. I know he will—but in his own sweet way, in his own sweet time. Do I have the strength to wait for his deliverance?

I have lived without money, without a home, without food even for ungodly periods of time. I have never been able to live for long without love. If I must do without your love I am doomed, for there is no one who can take your place. I have offered you my heart and with it the last shred of masculine pride. Trample it under foot, if you like, but do it with dispatch, I beg you.

I have loved you desperately, I still love you. I will love you till

Hell freezes over. Kill me with one blow, if it must be that way, and then I will know that you are really my "friend forever".

Your
Henry-San

/\.\/\.\/\.\/\.\

12/8/66

Dear, dear Hoki—

Tonight I am crazy with joy. I feel, I *know* you love me. I am thinking seriously about marriage. The only reason I don't propose immediately is because I want *you* to be sure you would not regret it. If you will come and live with me we would soon know if we are suited to one another. I feel that though you are now 29 years old you are still young and inexperienced. I wouldn't want to disappoint you. I want only to make you happy, to help you become the woman you would like to be. We have different temperaments, different interests, maybe different roads to travel. That is why I keep thinking of living a sort of trial marriage first. I am thinking mainly of *you*. I want you to have a fair chance. I am nearing the end of my life, and you are still at the beginning. I not only love you, I respect you, I honor you. I don't want to hurt you. Could we not try living together for a while before we make the final decision? Please believe I have only the tenderest feelings for you. If we could live together harmoniously, if I felt you were truly happy and fulfilled, nothing would give me greater happiness than to ask you to be my wife. And, whether you said it or not, you would be my last one!

Think it over. Be honest, as you usually are.

Henry-San
"The time of the hyena is upon us."*

* A quotation on the bottom of Henry's private stationery.—*Ed.*

/\./\./\./\./\./\

12/14/66

Dear Hoki-San—

We probably won't have much chance to talk this evening. How about dinner with me alone Friday evening, either here at the Gardens or at Patrone's Italian Restaurant—829 N. L. Cienega (you were there once for a wedding celebration.) If you decide on Patrone's, make it 6.45 P.M. so that we can have plenty of time. Let me know which!

I don't celebrate Xmas. I don't even give gifts or send cards. But you will be getting a gift, probably after Xmas, from Bogota, Colombia (South America). I don't know what it will be. I asked one of my fans there to select something she thought would please a charming, young, slightly spoiled Japanese woman.

I enjoyed reading your thoughts while I was in bed with a cold. It's lucky that I'm a mindreader!

Your
Henry-San

/\./\./\./\./\./\

Dec. 1966 4oc A.M.
(The hour of the
biting Crab)

Hoki, my dear—

Can't sleep. Toss around in bed thinking of you. The crab bites my toe. Are you awake, I wonder—or sound asleep? Another week-end—Sat. Sun. Monday—and you are again too busy to see me.

FALLING IN LOVE

Drives me mad. If the Queen of England, or better yet, Sophia Loren came to see me, and *you* asked to see me, I would make some excuse and find a way to be with *you*. Maybe Japanese politeness doesn't permit such behavior towards a guest. Too bad for Japanese. How can a woman in love let so many days, weeks, months go by without spending any real time with the man she loves? Doesn't she have a heart? Can't she ever break loose from the prison of convention? Or, doesn't she want to?

I feel like running away somewhere. I want to get free from this perpetual torment, this waiting, hoping, begging for little favors.

Yes, I admit that every moment I spend with you is precious to me. But it's always for a brief moment, it seems, and then Henry-San must wait again—and this waiting stretches out like an eternity. I am like a man suspended between Heaven and Hell. My real life is paralyzed. Oh yes, I have plenty to do, I can keep myself occupied, I can even pretend to enjoy the company of other women. But it's all meaningless. No matter where I am, whom I am with, my thoughts are always with you. Sometimes I am so absorbed in thoughts of you, longing for you, that I forget the name of the person I am with. I am only half there! The other half of me, the half that is truly me, is with you, talking to you, wondering about you.

The other night, after our good day together in Little Tokyo, I came home and wrote you a long letter. Then, I didn't send it. I waited to hear from you—just a little word to say maybe that you too had enjoyed yourself and hope to see me soon again. But no— just silence. Then I send a telegram, asking if you would keep Wednesday open for me. Again silence. (Tonight you tell me that you thought I would call you. One of our little misunderstandings.) So it goes. Maybe by January things will be better, easier, more convenient. But by January I can die a thousand deaths. I am doomed to live, in that "floating world", as the Japanese call it. I call it—Hell. It is a world in which Hoki appears now and then, like a vision. If I try to reach her, touch her, she vanishes like the early morning mist. And I am left staring into space with a thousand eyes, blind eyes, baffled eyes, hungry eyes.

And in spite of my anguish, in spite of my sickness—"my Japanese sickness" I call it—every one tells me I look fine, healthy, happy, carefree. "How do you do it?" they ask. I want to answer— "find someone to love . . . love till it hurts . . . turn yourself inside out, don't think about God, work, duty, just love till it drives you mad. Then, you will look fresh and rosy, and everyone will envy you, though your heart is torn to shreds."

But all I really say is—"How nice! Thank you! God is good to me." I play the clown or the angel or the man of wisdom, whatever suits the occasion best. And inside me I am weeping. How can a creature like Hoki-San make me suffer so? Ah yes, she is lovely, very lovely—and bewitching. Everyone I bring to the bar tells me the same thing—even the women! Tonight it was Duke's sister who was telling me these wonderful things about you. Finally I had to say to her—"Yes, I know all that. I know how lovely, how charming she is. Who doesn't?" And then I couldn't resist it—I said "I am madly in love with her!" Maybe she was a little drunk (?) I wished that I too were drunk, because I wanted to shout out loud: "I love her, I love her!" I wanted everybody to hear it, to know it. But I kept my mouth shut. As we were driving Nola home, I whispered in her ear—"Do you really think she loves me?" I was a little boy again. I needed to hear someone say—"Henry, your Hoki loves you. I am sure of it."

You asked me the other day, and you asked Nola—"Why doesn't he tell *me*?" As if I hadn't told you in a hundred different ways!!! Sometimes I think it is *because* you know I love you so much that you take advantage of me, play with me, *pretend* to be indifferent, or *pretend* to be jealous. You play it cool. Why? To be more certain that I love you, *only you*? Don't you *know* when some one loves you with all his heart and soul? Are you afraid of love?

I give up. It is 5.30 in the morning. I am dog tired. I am like a woman who is about to have her period. I am getting ready to bleed —and not just between the legs, but from every pore of my body . . . Let me say in closing that your piano playing is becoming more and more remarkable. I am aware of every modulation you make. Please now modulate into the key of love—and stay there. Do this for your

Henry-San

whose life is nothing

but a dream of love.

Good night!

/\.V.\/\.V.\/\.V.\

1/3/67

My dear Hoki—

After that good honest talk at the dinner table this evening, I realize that all is hopeless between us. I am not angry with you nor will I try to hurt you in any way. I couldn't, even if I wanted to, because despite everything I love you and it will take me a long time to get over it.

I admire you for being so frank and truthful. You can't help being what you are. I only regret that my love was not strong enough to overcome your weaknesses.

I can't live without love, foolish as that may sound to you. So I must seek happiness elsewhere, though it breaks my heart to do so.

For the love you inspired in me I thank you from the bottom of my heart. Even though it was disastrous it made me a richer human being. The pity of it is that you did not allow me to make something more of *you*.

If you are ever in distress I hope you will call on me, for I am always your friend, if nothing more.

Henry-San

/\\./\\./\\./\\./\\./\\./\\.\\

My dear Hoki—

I wrote the enclosed last night on coming home from the Imperial Gardens. On rereading it this morning I feel like adding a few more words, because I owe it to you to make things as clear as possible, and especially not to hurt you, not to make you feel guilty, or not to feel sorry for me.

You know that I have written you quite a few letters which I have never mailed. Some of them I destroyed, some I kept. I have not the heart to destroy these which I kept. I will send them to you if you wish, and you may destroy them yourself, for they really belong to you. When you read them, if you ever do, you will see what torment I have suffered because of my unrequited love for you.

What pains me in deciding to give up the battle is my own failure, as it were to live up to the full meaning of love, as expressed in that little book I gave you: "The Greatest Thing in the World". I am only human; I am weak. I expected my love to be returned; I expected my prayers to be answered. If I were a bigger man, a greater soul, I would have expected nothing in return; I would have asked only to keep on loving you, no matter what.

But being thoroughly human, how could you expect me to do this when you yourself confess that you don't love, can't love, do not know what love is—and more than that even, that you admit that you would be bored to death living with a man, sleeping with him, acting the wife or mistress, and so on and so on.

To love means to accept someone for what he or she is, and as I said above, I must reproach myself for my inability to do this. You presented yourself to me, in your moments of frankness, not as a person, not even as a human being, let alone a woman, but as a non-entity. How else could I react in the face of such admission?

Near the end of our talk you looked at me with your strange and haunting smile and you said: "You know, you have lasted longer than any of the other men I knew." The implication was—what is the matter with you, Henry? When are you going to wake up? When are you going to realize that I am no good for you, that you are just wasting time?"

I want you to know, dear Hoki, that all the thought, the attention, the love I felt for you was *not* wasted . . . *not for me.* And this is the one thing, I suppose, that you will never understand, that in giving oneself, no matter to whom, one gains, not loses, one is enriched, not impoverished.

In writing to you as I do today I know that I am not going to be cured of this love for you immediately. I only wish I could be. You leave a precious wound in me which it will take a long time to heal.

Tonight, as you know, I am to plead a lost cause for my friend Jean. I will talk to this woman as if I were talking to you, as if I were pleading for my own self. Maybe the miracle will happen, and she will melt, relent. Maybe I can do for him, Jean, what I cannot do for myself.

You introduced me to a number of your good friends. I want to tell you that some of them tried their best to help me. Others felt sorry for me, or pitied me. You *do* have good friends, and I know you yourself are a good friend. Your friends know you, understand you, and accept you for what you are. And I, who love you so much, am unable to do so. What a pity! What cruel misfortune!

I know you will forgive me and forget me easily. It's *you* who wanted it this way. Maybe in another reincarnation we will do better, you and I.

And now, do you know what I think would be a delicious way to end it all? Write a line to the editor of that Womans' Journal in Tokyo, saying that after mature deliberation and consideration Hoki Tokuda would like to announce to the world that she has renounced any thought of marriage with Henry Miller, that she intends to live her own life in her own way, regardless of the consequences.

As for Henry Miller, he will continue to go his own foolish way, believing in love, believing in the powers that be, believing in miracles.

If there is a Creator who is capable of giving us faith and joy, courage and good fortune, I beg him or it to bestow his favors on you, my dear Hoki. And again I say—"Thank you for having caused me to love you, even though it was all in vain!"

/\.\/\.\/\.\/\.\/\.\/\.\

Jan. 25th 1967

Dear Hoki-San,

I have just had a letter from the astrologer (Mme Langman) in Switzerland, asking about you. Like Mme Camargo in Columbia, she is very interested in you.

Now she writes that if you cannot give the hour of your birth, please try to give her the approximate dates (month and year) of the crucial periods of your life—from as far back as you can remember. She means, of course, events that marked you—like, perhaps, mother's death, first love (if painful), beginning of career, trips abroad, anything which deeply affected you emotionally.

Maybe, while you are resting—vacationing—some of these moments will come to mind. Why not jot them down in your notebook and give me them later?

Even if *you* are not interested in your own horoscope, *I am*. It would perhaps clear up a lot of things about you that now mystify me, at least where you and I are concerned.

You don't need to hand *me* this data, I can give you this woman's address and you can mail it to her yourself.

I forgot to tell you how this information helps the astronomer discover (approximately) the hour of birth—or sometimes the *exact* hour. (I had my own horoscope "corrected" twice by different astrologers. Mothers sometimes give wrong time—mine wasn't sure —only guessed at it.)

The point is that these main events in your life would show up clearly in your horoscope. They would be like reference points. But

44

I won't complicate it further. Please believe that I know what I'm talking about.

This woman, incidentally, is a most intuitive person. She seems to have a secret touch which is so important in the art of interpretation. I won't say any more. It is up to you now.

Just had a post card from Nobuko. That girl is an angel. Give her warm greetings for me, won't you please.

And take good care of yourself!

Your
Henry-San

P.S. "Town" with Tonoyama interview (and photos) is out—but I haven't received a copy yet. I am very curious to see what Tonoyama wrote.

ᐱᐱᐱᐱᐱᐱ
⚹·⚹·⚹·⚹·⚹·⚹

Jan. 28th 1967
3.15 A.M.

Hoki-San,

You grow more and more impossible. You behave like a child. It disgusts me. I wasn't drunk tonight, though I had plenty to drink. I was in a good mood. And you give me this nonsense about being mad, *I* should call you and so on. I refuse to play that game any more. I've had enough of it. Either you act like a woman or step out of my life entirely.

That I love you in spite of everything I can't deny, but I won't be treated like an idiot. I'll give you up even if it kills me.

And I don't want to hear you say "I'm sorry, I was in a bad mood, I had a headache," etc. etc. If you want me you will have to come to me, show me some affection, open your heart, prove to me that you love me. I won't accept anything less. I have offered you

45

everything and you have spurned it. I don't want any favors of you, I want *you*. And if you can't give yourself then I'm through.

I expect an answer. That's the least you can do. It's got to end one way or the other. I leave it to you to decide. Believe me, I'm in earnest.

Henry-San

/\\./\\./\\./\\./\\.\

February 1967

Dear Hoki-San—

Did Riko give you my message? I'm serious. No more games, no more play-acting. I'm going to Japan in late April. If you have to go back now I will see you there. I will marry you there, if you want me, if you really care for me. If you can remain here, I'll marry you here. It's up to you now. You have kept me guessing for many months. You've treated me shamefully. If I didn't love you so much as I do I would hate you.

This is the last time I talk about love—and marriage. If you don't answer I will understand that you are not interested. And then I will leave you alone, I will never bother you, never see you again.

If you feel like it, call me up tonight when you get home from work. I will be awake.

I want you to tell me the truth. If you feel I am too old for you, I will understand. If you are in love with someone else, I will understand. I wouldn't ask anything of you except what you freely wish to give.

Somebody was translating for me Tonoyama's article in "Town." I never said I wanted to sleep with a geisha, I would like to be a friend of one, not a lover, I didn't like the *tone* of this interview— it was too much like Playboy Magazine in America.

Henry-San

FALLING IN LOVE

∧∧∧∧∧∧∧
˙v˙v˙v˙v˙v˙v˙v˙

Tuesday (February)

Dear Hoki-San—

If you ever have stomach trouble again ask Frank to give you a *small*—very small—glass of Fernet-Branca. It is an Italian "digestif"—and works like magic. Tastes bitter, like medicine—but not *too* bad! Writing you to the Gardens so that if you still have the cramps you can get the drink tonight.

Dear Hoki—I can't make it to Hawaii after all. (You had just about persuaded me last night.) But now several unexpected things have come up, which obliges me to stay here—to my regret. Visits concerning my film—looks like Cantiflas (Mexican Chaplin) may take it. Doubleday (publisher) wants to photograph my paintings and talk to me—hope to do big album—30 to 40 water colors—for me. Have to meet conductor of L.A. Symphony—is interested in getting my opera produced in the U.S.A. *And* other things too— all over the weekend and early next week.

All of a sudden, when I no longer care what happens, things are breaking for me, just as my Swiss astrologer predicted for 1967. If I don't die in Japan, maybe it will be a good year for me and I will live to enjoy the fruits of my labor, as they say.

If I don't see you before you leave for Hawaii do have a wonderful time! And be careful of eating ripe, tropical fruits—or you may have more stomach ache! (*Pineapple fresh* should be great!)

I'll miss you. But then I miss you here too.

Henry-San

P.S. I gave you the records not because of the singing so much but because of the words I marked off. Especially "Domino." When I come again I wish you would sing it for me.

47

/\/\/\/\/\/\/\

2/2/67

Dear Hoki—

This is the last sleepless night because of Hoki Tokuda. I've decided at long last to forget you, to put you out of my mind, bury you once and for all. The reason shouldn't be hard to guess. You have only to consult your real feelings about me.

For a moment, when you were speaking to me on the phone, urging me to go to Hawaii with you, I thought I detected a note of genuine tenderness, genuine desire, in your voice. And it melted me.

But in my heart I know you don't really care for me. I believe now all the terrible things you have told me about yourself. Suddenly it dawns on me there is nothing to hope for between us. There never was anything—except for my foolish dreams. I had hoped to have a good talk with you, to settle certain things, at least in my own mind. My intuition tells me I would get nowhere with you. You would only leave me sitting on the fence, as you have these many months.

If it hurts you to read these words, believe me, it hurts me a thousand times more. But I must make an end of it or you will destroy me. You have already humiliated me as a man. I endured that because I was crazy enough to think that my love would overcome everything. But I have come to the conclusion, right or wrong, that nothing, absolutely nothing, can affect you deeply. You have put yourself beyond the reach of love, whether man's love or God's love. One day you may wake up. Let us hope it will not be too late.

Henry-San

FALLING IN LOVE

∧∧∧∧∧∧∧

April, 1967 Sat. 10:10 P.M.
Hour of the Scorpion
Month of the Cobra
Year of desperation

Hoki-Sama:

This is another crazy letter, perhaps the last one. To begin with I am tired, very, very tired, not only because I have had no decent rest for over eight weeks, not only because I have been burning the candles at both ends, but mainly because I get so little real response from you. I don't know how much longer I can hold out. In all my life you are the only woman who has treated me with such indifference. You don't even hate me, which would be a sign of some feeling. You behave as if I did not exist, or as if I existed like some pendant you wear around your neck. When I telephone you you tell me about the laundromat and how classy a Jaguar is, but never one extra word which might betray any human emotion, any warmth, any desire, any enthusiasm. Any crumb of affection I have to read in your eyes. But if I stay long enough at the bar I may find the same look being given to Mr. Nobody or Mr. Anybody. It is the look of the entertainer who feels she must please her public. No one gets special attention, or so it seems. I know I'm talking like a jealous egotist. But I can't help it. I am not that way naturally. Normally I am trusting and believing, I have faith in people. As I said before, it's the feeling you give of no response which drives me crazy. You never show the slightest interest, the slightest curiosity, about anything I tell you or write about. It's as though I were throwing my words into a cement mixer.

I know that you are not a letter writer. I know you cannot express yourself in English as you would like to, and yet, if you really wished to communicate you could. I have had real communication with people who knew far less English than you, whose language was

49

often ridiculous, but who managed to convey their feelings nevertheless. Sometimes I wonder if it is because I do not understand Japanese women that I have such difficulties with you. But then, are Japanese women really so different from all other women in this world? Are they really so inscrutable? After all, you are of the new generation; you are a modern Japanese woman, you are independent, you earn your own living, you solve your own problems. I am not dealing with a woman of the Meiji period. Lady Murasaki is quite understandable to me, though she lived almost a thousand years ago. Why should Hoki offer such a problem?

And then I think—perhaps like other women she has not told me the whole truth about herself. Perhaps she is in love with some other man, and does not tell me for fear of hurting my feelings. Perhaps she values my friendship more than my love. Maybe this is Japanese tact, Japanese discretion, Japanese kindness—and I am too stupid to understand or appreciate it.

And then another thought comes to mind, one which I want to forget. We were sitting at the table in your house, and we were talking of love, when suddenly from your lips came something like this: "I too felt that way when I was younger, but I have gotten over all that"—as if it (love) was all so much nonsense. I remember your putting your hand out to congratulate me (ironically) for having had several proposals of marriage. As if to say, "how nice to be still so romantic, at your age!" The implication being that you had turned your back on all that, that there were other more important, more exciting things in life than just being in love.

Anyway I am utterly confused, utterly bewildered. In my enthusiasm I send you things from my readers which I think may arouse a spark of curiosity, but they fall on the ground like dead autumn leaves. And then I am embarrassed. Does she think, I ask myself, that I am trying to build myself up, prove that I am this or that? How silly, how dreadful that would be. The truth is I have no one to share with me all the wonderful things that come to me in the mail. And I need to share these things with someone. Otherwise I would be like a miser counting his hoard. Which reminds me of my secretary, Connie, who has been with me now for about two years. Gems pass through her hands every day, but she never recognizes them. In all this time, she has never read a book of mine; she has filed a thousand letters or more and never bothered, out of curiosity, to read a single one, never wanted to know who this person or that was, why they wrote such a letter. She is willing, obedient, at my beck and call, whether it is to write a letter, answer the phone, drive me anywhere, or wash the toilet bowl. I think if I said to her—"Connie, would you please raise your dress and show me your cunt," she would do it. In other words one thing is no more important to her than another. It's all in a day's work. "At your service, Master" seems to be her motto. Maybe some people would consider her the perfect secretary. Not me! It drives me crazy, though I appreciate all she is willing to do for me. I don't want a robot for a secretary, I want a human being.

Or, as Ueno-San writes me at the end of his last letter: "May you be more crazy in this love, and so become so much younger. Forget everything and throw yourself into the fire of love until the fire melts you. I like burning love, dynamic love, terrible love! Life losing love! Harakiri love, Kamikaze love. Love as a rosy crucifixion, is no one's but yours. Hallelujah! Amen!" So speaks a descendent of the Samurai. And I, who imagine that my ancestors were Mongols, Huns, Tartars, echo his words.

Maybe this Ueno-San is a very eccentric person, a very strange Japanese, and I am sure he is! But what life breathes through his letters, what enthusiasm, what a desire to know and share my thoughts. There he is, five thousand miles away, in a God-forsaken town called Ichinosaki (Iwate Prefecture), and yet it is as if he were living just around the corner from me. Every week two or three letters, magazines, drawings by his children, little gifts of one kind or another. And a thousand questions as he reads one of my books after another. And you, whom I love, you who are only a few miles away from me, you whom I bombard with letters, to whom I pour out my heart . . . well, you might be living in the Gobi desert for all it matters. Or on the planet Jupiter. You talk about me you say.

But do you talk *to* me? Maybe you do in your sleep. But even that I doubt, having seen how soundly you sleep, how like an Easter Island head your night face is.

What strange, wonderful, mixed emotions I felt the last time I slept in your bed! How I wanted to squeeze you to death, talk to you, get under your skin, establish some real contact, some tangible human closeness! When you said "I feel so weak", I was ready to fall apart. I felt such tenderness, such a desire to comfort you, protect you, give you strength—to even think of making love to you seemed like committing sacrilege. How could I dare to express my passion for you when what you needed was something greater, something above and beyond that? I felt for you then so much more than a man usually feels for a woman. I intended, after I was sure you had fallen fast asleep, to get up quietly and dress, then sneak out of the house and walk down to Sunset Boulevard. I wanted to leave you in peace, leave you to rest undisturbed. But then you happened to turn your face to me and in the dim light I became fascinated by what I saw—that night face whose image will never, never leave me. I just couldn't go.

Well, my dear, dear Hoki, if you have read this far you must have some idea of the torment I am going through. As I said in the beginning, perhaps this will be the last such letter I shall write you. It is up to you now to decide what our future relationship will be like. If you want it to end, all you need to do is to ignore this letter as you have all the others. That will be sufficient answer, and will cost you no effort. If that is how you want it to be I promise you I won't bother you any more . . . I'll never write again, nor telephone, nor, with God's help, see you again. It will take every ounce of courage and strength I possess, but I will do it. If necessary I will go away somewhere, Europe, anywhere, until the wound is healed. Whatever happens I shall never forget you, never stop loving you.

And so, sweet Princess, good-night!

FALLING IN LOVE

/\\/\\.\\/\\.\\/\\.\\/\\

Dear Hoki-San,

Riko-San told me this morning what good things you said about
me to Mako's friend. I was very much touched. As you know, even
if you were to become my enemy one day I would only be able to
speak well of you. And especially of your "soul", which means
"Hoki" in Armenian, I learned recently.

I had two letters from Japan yesterday, telling me about that
article in Playboy. It seems they have given a lot of attention to
Fugishima's words—which is too bad. I feel that he must be some
kind of malicious idiot!

Connie is trying to get address of Harper and Row, so that we
can find out if translation rights for the Japanese language are still
available.

Do you know something—I would like to write your father a
letter. I want to tell him some good things about you and also that
I hope to meet him when I go to Japan—maybe in October. Could
you give me his address and the name of his business firm? (I
would show you my letter before I mailed it to him.)

I have attacks of insomnia now and then, but this time it is different. I wake up smiling or laughing, my heart filled with joy.
Isn't that wonderful? And I owe it all to *you*. I lost out as "the great
lover", but I found myself as a man, as a human being who is
content just to live and does not need to ask the gods or any one
for favors, I just thank God (or whomever!) for being alive and
able to enjoy his creation.

By the way, did that young girl from Tokyo, who wanted to work
in America—Miss Matsunaga—ever arrive? I still have her photo.
And I will have some photos of you at the opening of the show. I
may give the whole series to Riko tonight.

Aishite ru!*

Henry-San

* "Love forever!"

53

/\/\.\/\.\/\.\/\.\/\

copy for Hoki-San   *June 10, 1967*
Dear Atsu-San—*Atsu Kawabata*

After all the talks we had I still feel as if there were more to tell
you, but honestly don't know where to begin—or stop. (I suppose
I shall have to write it all out myself one day, as I told you.) My
main concern at the moment is that justice should be rendered to
Hoki. I don't mind at all if I am made to look like a fool, and an
old fool at that, than which there is nothing worse, as you know. If
you have read the life of Goethe you will understand what I am
hinting at. That last affair of his, with the young girl who rejected
him, remains forever in my memory. However, we have the other
side of the picture in the life of Pablo Casals who at ninety has been
happily married for eight or nine years with a woman who is only
thirty today. But then Casals is one of the rare human spirits of this
day and age. He is probably the only man in the world whose way
of life I envy, and not because of his successful love but because of
everything he does and says, his devotion to his art, his marvelous
fight for his countrymen, and so on. . . .

With all that I told you about Hoki and myself I realize that there
is a shadowy aspect to the real nature of the "drama". In all my
books, and even in the case of Mona, whom I portrayed more fully
and vividly than the others, I have been reluctant to dwell on the
true nature of "love"—perhaps because I feel that it is sacred and
of no concern to the public, and partly because this kind of love
should be spelled with a capital L—LOVE, not what goes by that
name generally. At bottom I have a secretive nature, especially
about those things which are of vital importance to me. I can tell
anecdotes easily, and I can parody myself and others, I can lie,
invent, distort, amuse, but when it comes down to the real facts, the
real feelings, I am very shy and reticent, and communicate only
with my "guardian angel", so to speak. So, let me repeat, in spite

54

of all the seeming confessions I have made throughout my works, my real self, my real adventures, remain hidden.

What complicated the Hoki "romance" was my ignorance and ineptitude with reference to Oriental women, the Japanese woman in particular. I did not know, for a long time, for instance, that one does not say "I love you" to a Japanese woman—at least, not until the right moment. I know, of course, that the Western man, and especially the American, uses the word love too lightly. In my case it was sincere, genuine, and I think Hoki eventually came to realize that. Another difficulty, or blunder on my part, was that I did not realize that it was an insult to ask a Japanese woman to live with one without being married. I took Hoki to be a very modern girl, even though raised in Japan. Then too, as I told you, she had made it very clear to me from the beginning that she was not interested in marriage. The very thought of marriage seemed to frighten her. Here let me repeat what I said to you several times—that Hoki was always truthful, sincere, honest with me. She told me all her faults and shortcomings, which I found difficult to believe. Perhaps she did so to discourage me. But I respected her for being so frank, and I might add, I loved her all the more for telling me the truth.

And now, as I relate this, I feel impelled to add a few words off the record, about love and marriage. I think that love, especially with a capital L, is one thing, and marriage another. You know very well that I don't believe in marriage as it exists today. And yet there is such a thing as "marriage", whether it is legal or illegal. And there most certainly can be love, whether it is ever consummated by marriage or not. Marriages are made in heaven, as I said somewhere. Such marriages are between two "souls". There may be physical union and there may not be, it makes no difference. Maybe what I am referring to comes under the head of what Goethe called "elective affinities".

Speaking of love, this kind of love, this attraction of two souls despite all the handicaps and barriers of race, religion, upbringing, and so on, what difference does it make if the woman one loves be a cabaret dancer, a whore, a thief or whatever? Hoki might have been any of these things, and it would not have altered my love for her in the least. Perhaps it would even have added something to my passion—an element of compassion, of a desire to aid and protect, of a challenge for deeper understanding.

The disparity in our age, in our status (?), and all that is, of course, what intrigues the Japanese reader. But why can they not view all this as proof of something rare and beautiful instead of trivial and ridiculous? Frankly, I do not care what the Japanese public thinks of me. I stand on my record. And, if I am truly blind, foolish, deluded, what of it? I am that much more human, is it not so? We are not living in a world of gods and demi-gods, but of human beings who are good and bad, wise and ignorant, gentle and vicious.

Well, I think I have said more than enough. I am trying to get you some interesting photos but both my friends are frightfully busy and I may not have them for several days yet. I'll send them on to you as soon as they are ready. Some of these photos of Hoki, particularly those taken at the gallery recently, are strikingly beautiful and show her up at her loveliest.

If there is anything more I can do for you please let me know. I can't tell you what a pleasure it was to meet you. And once again I must compliment you on your use of English. You are the first Japanese I ever heard speak it so fluently and correctly—and with no accent! My best to you always!

Sincerely,
HM

/\.\.\.\.\.\.\

June 20th 1967

To the Japanese Reading Public

Now that most of the dirty linen has been washed in public it gives me pleasure to wash a few dirty socks and handkerchiefs myself. I don't promise to tell the whole truth, because that's nobody's business but my own. I would simply like to relate a few homely facts about the notorious Miller-Tokuda romance which have been overlooked or distorted by the numerous reporters at large who have made it their business to keep the pot boiling at any cost.

It is true that I have been, and perhaps still am, madly in love with Hoki Tokuda, late of the Imperial Gardens, Hollywood. According to the last bulletin from Tokyo the affair is now ended. Also, according to that same dispatch, I recently bought an art gallery for our mutual friend Riko Mizuno. And in that same report it was said that Riko Mizuno had to translate my love letters to Hoki-San because the latter's knowledge of English was too limited. In other reports I have read that the water colors I gave Hoki-San were worth $30,000.00—not yen! No one has yet told about the stone from King Solomon's mine which I also gave Hoki-San and from which we had two rings made, nor of the mansion in Beverly Hills which I am contemplating buying for her just to prove that we are still good friends. Nor have I heard a word about the Rolls Royce I have selected for her in the event that she marries an Oriental potentate.

No, I did not buy an art gallery for Riko Mizuno though I would gladly have done so if she had asked me. Instead I was honored by her with an exhibition of my paintings to celebrate the opening of her almost famous gallery. Nor did Riko Mizuno have to translate my love letters to Hoki-San, first because Hoki knows more English than Riko-San, and second because even if I had written these letters in Turkish or Swahili the thoughts conveyed were so transparent that even "a Japanese playgirl" could understand them. It was I who had to get Hoki-San's letters translated, because my Japanese is almost nil. Nor was this a difficult matter, since I received only one and a half letters from Hoki-San during this entire period. What is giving me real grief at the moment is the translation of Lady Nogi's letter of instruction to her niece. In this beautiful piece of wisdom stemming from the Meiji period I have encountered a number of locutions which are no longer employed in Japanese today.

If any one wonders why I am concerned with Lady Nogi's sentiments about the proper conduct of a wife please know that I regard her words as a recipe for a successful marriage. Further, when I am satisfied with the translation I shall copy it out in my best handwriting, frame it, and put it over my bed. Thus, when the happy day comes that I marry again I shall be able to say to my bride— "Please to read carefully and follow to the letter!"

It is hardly necessary to add that, aside from all the other reasons Hoki-San may have had for not wishing to marry an old goat like Henry Miller, the aforesaid rules of conduct would definitely have taken the wind out of her sails.

Though it would seem that the "romance" is ended the truth is that it has only begun. That is, on my part. And the reason is that I was born a Capricorn—and time is always on our side. The symbol for this sign, as every one knows, is that of a mountain goat, a chamois, let's say, which slowly, slowly climbs to the heights, browsing as he goes along. Or another way of putting it would be— the image of a man with feet securely buried in the earth and the wings of an angel flapping in the wind. In other words, a creature whose goal is heavenward but who never loses touch with reality. He will get there, even if it takes a thousand years. And so, though I am not yet dead to the earth, I have begun the second round, praying that in my next incarnation I will be forty years younger when I meet the loved one, more handsome, more seductive, perhaps less intelligent, less talented, but not lacking in *Jo* and *Iro*.

Though the old goat has been rejected, and properly so, though he is temporarily out of the race, he is still permitted the privilege of seeing the lost one, of holding her hand now and then, of sending flowers and telegrams when the spirit moves him, and so on. All the little amenities, in short, which prove that the damage is not irreparable. The *Tonogo* is still living in the world of his *Okugata*, still filled with that old-fashioned *cho-ai* which is so becoming to his years. One romance begins, another ends, but love goes on forever.

Henry Miller

FALLING IN LOVE

/\/\.\/\./\/\./\/\.\

7/3/67

Dear Hoki-San—

I know you will think me foolish to have written such a letter to
Kawabata-San, but that's the way I am and I cannot change. I do
not send you this copy of my letter to impress you with my unending
love, because, to use Riko's words, we know that Hoki doesn't give
a shit. (But Hoki *does*, I know, even if she pretends differently.)

Today, as Riko may have told you, I received the Japanese
weekly with article written by your brother-in-law. I see a photo of
your father, who looks good to me, and a lovely one of you when
you were younger. I have the pages for you.

Warm greetings to Fumiko who really is an enchanting person.

As Shakespeare says—"All's well that ends well." (Whatever that
means!)

Je t'embrasse.

Henry-San

/\/\.\/\./\/\./\/\.\

copy for Hoki-San   *July 3rd, 1967*

Dear Mr. Kawabata—dear Atsu-San:

Only today did I manage to hear the whole of the tape you made
for me of your translation. I want to thank you for having taken
so much trouble on my behalf. And also to let you know I bear you
no ill will. Evidently your effort to put an end to the gossip about
Hoki and myself has not succeeded. More articles seem to be ap-
pearing in Japanese magazines. Naturally, the Japanese journalists
will make the most of this juicy material, and in doing so are no

worse than other journalists the world over. I am beginning to take it all as a huge joke, wondering how far and how long it will go on.

Hoki and Riko both were disappointed, as you know. I think the mistake you made was to inquire about Hoki from those who knew her. If you had confined your text to your interview with me things would have turned out more smoothly. I myself could not see what purpose it served to discuss Hoki's earnings which I think are exaggerated. And it is not true that Hoki asked me to buy her the Jaguar, nor did I buy it! Hoki has never asked me for money; on the contrary, she has made me gifts of all kinds. And I have done likewise, to be sure. It hurt her to be referred to as a "shicho"(?). And perhaps even more that you said Riko had to translate my letters because Hoki did not understand English well enough. It's the other way round—Riko knows less English than Hoki. I tried to understand what you explained about my "presenting Riko with the gallery", which I did not do, of course. To begin with, Riko would never have accepted such a gift of me. The monies I laid out for the opening of the gallery were all expenses that any artist would ordinarily be asked to pay by the gallery presenting his work. I knew Riko did not have such money, so I volunteered to shell out for her. She insists on paying it back. (I believe about the Japanese people that they never ask favors, especially of a foreigner even if he is a friend. I think they are more scrupulous in this respect than most any other people.)

The strange thing about all these articles concerning Hoki and myself is this—why should the Japanese writers run Hoki down, one of their own people? They all give the impression of being sorry for me, the great writer. They make it appear as if I had chosen a Japanese woman who was unworthy of my love. In a way, all this is very flattering, I mean this desire to come to my rescue. But it is not necessary. I walked into this affair with eyes wide open. Hoki herself, as I told you before, warned me about herself. Not that she made herself out to be a cheap woman, but simply trying to tell me that I was not to see things in her which she did not possess, nor expect of her things she could not offer. I don't think a "shicho" girl would have acted in this manner. In short, she promised me nothing. But enough of this. . . . Why, I ask you, could not a Japanese writer see the beautiful side of this romance? There is so little real love in this world—why not talk about love? What love can do for a man, or a woman. Love is what makes the world go round, as the saying goes. Without love there is no life. And who should know this better than the Japanese, in whom love is fostered like a delicate plant?

I had to smile when you conjectured that the Japanese expressions I used in the Insomnia paintings were given me by Japanese friends. Not at all! I got them from a book called "The Cradle of Erotica". It has to do with the sex practices of Japanese, Chinese, Hindus, Arabs and Africans. The quotation which goes "When you enter the hall of love take off your shoes" is not mine either. I think I got it from Victor Hugo, as I did the one about "the slaughter-house of love" (meaning bordels). And you missed the point about "chin-chin", which is what we often say when raising a toast. In your language it means "prick", the vulgar expression for penis. I didn't know this until I toasted a Japanese friend at the Imperial Gardens one night—and every one laughed. And then about inviting people for ping pong Wednesday nights . . . You say I gathered common girls from the street and their boys friends—*and divorcees!* Ha ha! Ho ho! It's true that I never ask "intellectuals" on that night. I play ping pong because I am sick of hearing people discuss art and literature in my home. But I don't ask just anybody to come play ping pong. If anything, I try to get pretty girls (or women) and good players, that's all. I want to have some fun, nothing more.

I also wondered about the Mexican girl or woman you mention. Did *I* tell you that story? In the article it would appear that I couldn't get an erection ("mara"); on the tape you make it seem, at least to me, as if I was still too much in love with Hoki to make love to another woman. Let me clear this up for you. If it was the Mexican girl I told you about, the reason I couldn't do anything was because she was too young and didn't know how to take care of herself, or didn't care. But I can make love with a woman (over eighteen) and still love Hoki. I find that almost "Japanese", don't you? Or, to put it another way, Hoki-San did not castrate me (psychologically). Nor would she want to.

I am not naturally suspicious. In fact, as you have hinted, I am rather naive, almost "innocent". I don't believe you meant to hurt any one. I think you were trying to be sincere and helpful. Recently I have been reading a book you probably know—"The Chrysanthemum and the Sword" by Ruth Benedict. Reading this book, I realize how very very little I really know about the Japanese, about their mind, their way of thinking, and so on. And so, if I seem to be critical about some of the things you have written, please forget it. Consider me an ignorant Westerner who happens to love Japan and all she stands for but who will never penetrate the mystery of her ways.

The last thing . . . It was rather touching to read about that "mock" wedding ceremony you described, and somewhat inaccurate too, I believe. I don't think there was any one but Riko, Hoki and myself present. I don't think it took place in a restaurant either. As a matter of fact, I have forgotten a good deal of what actually took place, because I had built the situation up to such proportions in advance that when it did occur I was in a state of shock. You used the word "mock" when referring to Hoki's tears. But you, as a Japanese, should have appreciated that she could hardly have acted otherwise. What you overlook, I think, are Hoki's real feelings. You will never know them, nor I either, nor perhaps anybody, including her closest and dearest friend. Hoki is anything but what people think she is. She is even a mystery to herself! You may laugh at this, and think once again that it is the romantic, naive, child-like Henry Miller who is talking. But I am talking truth, and from knowledge. It's because I know Hoki-San so well that I love her and respect her and can forgive her anything—if she needs forgiveness.

My dear Atsu-San, I am running on like a wild duck, and you must forgive me for taking up so much of your time. I am now on my second gin and tonic and my tongue loosens up. All that I have written you I beg you to treat confidentially—and I know I can trust you. Listen to me a bit longer, please. I don't have any Japanese man-friend in whom I can confide or *would* confide. For all my loose talk I am truly a secretive person, as I told you previously.

This Hoki romance is not finished, believe me. It may be for Hoki, but not for me. I still love her. But I have ceased annoying her with my love. I know as well as she how hopeless it is. But I am a man moving toward the grave, and she is still a young girl with a life to live. I no longer feel hurt or wounded, nor bitter because I was rejected. I simply feel a great big empty hole in my life because she can not share my life with me. Perhaps she would make me miserable if she did accept me. Perhaps I would hate her eventually, if ever we were to live together. But this has nothing to do with my love. It is not Hoki who hurt me, but this love which is too big for my little heart. I am a free man, I can do what I like, love whom I like, and so on. But this does not make up for the absence of the one I love. Call me naive, if you will, but I believe that Hoki loves me—in the way that Hoki understands love. I am not ready to commit suicide yet, and probably never will, though I have tried several times. I would like to die now, if you want to know the truth, but it is not in my destiny to die yet. I am destined to live long, it seems, and the thought does not make me happy. I have had just about everything I wanted in this life, and looking back on my life, I find that the joy and the misery were equally good. But to live without love is something unbearable. If I had the Samurai spirit I would kill myself now. But I am not of the Samurai strain. I am "just a Brooklyn boy", as I have often said. No matter what you may think of Hoki, for me she symbolizes Japan. She is not a Lady Nogi, but for me she is nevertheless an Okugata. Too bad that I am not a Tonogo! And now I think I have said enough. Please consider me as your friend and next time you write about us make it more poetic, more unbelievable, more beautiful!

Sincerely,
H.M.

/\.\/\.\/\.\/\.\/\.\

July 18, 1967

Dear Hoki-San,

I'm very sorry to tell you that I won't be able to help you out with the house after all. A very dear old friend who is in desperate need has asked me for aid and I simply cannot refuse him. And I have no other cash at the moment. I hope you will forgive me.

Sincerely,

Henry-San

CUANDO MERDA TIVER VALOR POBRE NASCE SEM CU*

* Ed. Note: The last line is the new quotation printed on Henry's notepaper. This is Portuguese: "When shit has value the poor will be born without asses."

/\.\/\.\/\.\/\.\/\.\

8/14/67

Dear Hoki-San—

How do you feel today? Are you still unhappy?

I just got from the framer the pencil portrait you made of me. You will be surprised when you see it. When you sit down to eat at my table again you will see it.

I feel apologetic towards your lovely friend Izuni for not giving her more attention, but you saw what a crazy day it was.

I must also say I did not like the photos of you which Nancy Golden brought yesterday. The lighting was too harsh. Did not do you justice.

FALLING IN LOVE

"Aishite ru!"*

Justice! When are your compatriots going to do you justice? They treat you almost as bad as Pierre Loti did his Madame Chrysanthemum (Kikou). Or as she treated him—whichever way you like. But all this nonsense will one day take a different turn. Your day is coming. I hope it comes before you are an old lady.

Do you know that you look even lovelier when you weep a little? The mascara makes the tear drops turn black, which gives an interesting effect. But never cry too hard or you are apt to spoil the effect!

One of the strangest items in Ikeda's narrative was the yarn about your dream which finishes sitting on the toilet. If he invented that he is a surrealist!

I remember reading a story once called "Lady of Beauty" by Kikou Yamata in which this beautiful woman sends her lover some of her fresh *caca* in a beautiful enameled box—as a token of her affection. That's even more surrealistic, don't you think?

The Chinese aphrodisiac had no effect on me. Maybe I need to swallow it in big doses, or maybe I'm getting impotent. If so, that would solve a lot of problems, *non?*

I must stop now—dinner is ready. Maybe I'll see you for dinner one evening before the week is out.

Sleep well—and don't tell any one your dreams!

Love to Puko-San and a good hug for yourself.

Henry-San

P.S. Thank you again for the delicate stationery and the mobile! Did *you* leave the perfumed soap in my bathroom?

* "Love forever!"

65

/\.V.\.V.\.V.\

(copy for Hoki-San)   *August 18, 1967*
Dear Mr. Tokuda,

Once again I have to thank you warmly for your most kind and
most generous repeated invitation. I am sorry to be so late in re-
plying but due to preparations for my European trip I have been
literally standing on my head.

I understand very well indeed Mr. Takayama's desire to make
plans ahead of time and to get what information he can about my
exhibitions and other things. And I hope, before proceeding further,
that you will tell Mr. Takayama that I am deeply touched by his
evident sincerity and magnanimity. He must be a very unusual
individual.

But now let me try to explain myself to you, if I can. The older
I get the more I struggle *not* to make plans in advance, not to think
of tomorrow, or yesterday either, for that matter. I try my best to
live day to day, as we say in English. This is a result of my philo-
sophical strain rather than of my innate temperament. I have been
all my life a most active man, perhaps too much so. All I ever
wanted of life was the freedom to write what I had to express and
to do so with perfect freedom. It has been a long hard struggle, and
I suppose one might say that I won out. But at what a price! As a
result of my achievement, my fame or success, whatever you wish
to call it, the world tries to involve me in things which no longer
concern me. Every day of my life, for the last ten years or more, I
have to struggle to win a couple of hours which I may truly call my
own. The consequence of all this is that I do less and less creative
work. I am at the mercy of the world. And since my time on earth
is running short you can well understand how desperate I sometimes
feel. I have thought of running off to some remote corner of the
earth, where I might live in peace and do only what I wish to do,
but where is that place? Years ago I thought of going to Tibet or

to Nepal or some remote corner of India, but today I haven't the heart to pick myself up and go to such outlandish places. I need some comforts and also some medical attention. And I don't want to leave my son here alone should he be drafted into the military service.

I am telling you all this by way of explaining why I don't wish to make any definite plans for next Spring. By next Spring I may be dead, for one thing. Or I may have decided I want to go somewhere else. Or I may prefer to stay right here and do my traveling *"autour de ma chambre"*. I would probably have abandoned the European trip too were it not that my friend who engineered the trip (and exhibitions) would be terribly hurt. I shall have to go to Paris and Uppsala and Stockholm, even if it is in a wheel chair. I have committed myself and too many people are involved. I simply cannot disappoint them. But to tell you the truth, I wish I were back home already, sitting at my work table and quietly making fresh water colors.

You might tell Mr. Takayama that, to answer his queries,

1.) I would not know till the last minute how many paintings would be available; nor would I want to decide what price; nor bother with titles, size and all that. I never give titles any more— they mean nothing.

2.) I have on hand perhaps a hundred or more color prints of my work, largely recent work. I have had over a dozen important exhibitions, all over the world, but am not sure I still have the catalogs.

3.) It is not so important to me *where* I am exhibited; I would take a chance at the last minute. I don't attach such great importance to my paintings.

5.) I don't see any necessity for Mr. Takayama to deposit any guarantee money; I would trust him.

As for the book about Hoki-San, since I have not even begun it yet, I think we should let that wait. It is possible that in my contracts with the Japanese publishers I am already bound to submit to them my next work. However, I don't think this is so. I shan't begin to write about Hoki until I am in the right mood and circumstances are just right for me. I want to do it quietly, in great peace, and with all my heart. When that time will be God alone knows. I pray for it every day.

Well, I think I have taken up enough of your time. I hope I have made myself clear. You realize, no doubt, that I am a difficult person to deal with, difficult to pin down, I mean. But I hope you know that my heart is in the right place, that I deeply appreciate your efforts in my behalf, both yours and Mr. Takayama's, and that I feel as a friend toward you, if I may permit myself such a liberty.

I have seen your daughter a few times since my last letter and am happy to report that her spirit seems to grow brighter and clearer every day. I don't think she will ever be truly happy, but is that so important? The big thing is for her to find herself, I think. If I could help her do that I would consider that I had done her the greatest favor possible. All good wishes to you and to Madame Tokuda. I shall continue to write you from time to time.

Most sincerely yours,
H.M.

/.\/.\/.\/.\/.\/.\

8/23/67

Dear Hoki-San—

Here's the fifty I owe you. Better luck next time! If you go again to Las Vegas, introduce yourself to Carl Cohen, owner of the Sands. He's one of my fans. Offered to put me up free anytime I go there. I once told him I was coming there with you—but that was just before we "fell out". This is no "raba reta"!

Going to dinner in a few minutes with Omarr, Bricktop (the famous Negress with red hair) and two Japanese chicks. Friday night with Franchot Tone and Ben Gazzara—maybe Imperial Gardens. If it's early and you are free will you come?

Did I understand you to say your work visa does not permit you to work anywhere except in Japanese and Chinese establishments? Is that "absolute" or could a clever agent or lawyer have it changed, made more flexible?

Ima watachi-no kimtana achi desu.* (How's that for colloquial Japanese?)

Henry-San

P.S. Don't marry unless you can follow Madame Nogi's instructions!

* I've got a hard on.

8/30/67

Dear Hoki—

I just wrote a good, old friend—Paul Jacobs—who lives in San Francisco—about your case. He was very active for years in the Labor movement. Knows big people everywhere—in the political world. Has big job with Ford Foundation in Santa Barbara.

Because I may have to go to hospital any day I gave him your home telephone and Grand Star one (so he can contact you directly and quickly.) I explained as much as I could. I sent letter special delivery. Sometimes he travels, but his wife (who is a lawyer) would telephone him. I wrote on back of envelope for her to open the letter if he was not home.

I pray that this may help. Paul is real dynamite—and if anyone can get things done, I feel he can.

I am very nervous now as I dread thought of going to hospital—also of *not* going to Europe.

I will know in a day or two *what's what*.

I am also telephoning Dr. Siegel today about you. Couldn't get him last night.

May God be good to you!

Henry

Hoki dressed in her "native attire" as Henry called it.

Hoki in a museum, 1966.

Hoki performing at the Imperial Gardens, 1966.

Henry Miller, age three. The first three postcards Henry sent
to Hoki were of himself at age three.

The wedding in Beverly Hills, September 10, 1967.

The Millers at home, 1968.

Hoki and Henry, 1968.

Henry and Hoki at the
wedding license bureau.

Hoki posing for Henry, 1968.

Hoki performing on Japanese television, 1968.

Part II

MARRIAGE

On September 10, 1967, Hoki and Henry were married at the Beverly Hills home of Dr. Lee Siegel. The following week, they went to Paris for their honeymoon and an exhibition of Henry's water color paintings at the Galleries Gervais. They were joined in Paris by Henry's longtime friend, the author Lawrence Durrell.

Then they returned to their home in the Pacific Palisades.

In 1968, Hoki made three trips to Japan. The first, early in the year, was brief, to visit her father who was ill. Henry did not feel well enough to accompany her.

The second time she went to Japan was in April, to promote a large exhibition of Henry's paintings in Tokyo and other major cities. Both Hoki and the Japanese were disappointed when Henry declined to go.

The third visit back to her country was in September, to pursue her career. She was in a movie, did TV shows, recordings and radio work. She returned home early in November.

/\/\/\/\/\/\/\

October, 1967
Sunday night

Dear Hoki-San—

Just a little word to say that I think about you more and more every day. It seems to me that some sort of barrier between us has broken down. You seem happier, freer than before. Are we beginning to understand each other better?

I feel now how stupid and intolerant I was in criticizing you. I used to think that you thought only about yourself, about your little selfish pleasures. Now I see everything differently. I feel that you really are my wife, that you try to please me, make me happy.

Don't leave me alone too long, I need you.

Sleep well. Try to take a swim with me tomorrow. Yes?

Your
Henry-San

/\\/.\\/.\\/.\\/.\\/.\\/.\\/\

February, 1968
Saturday afternoon

The only real, valid, valuable and most precious gift you can give me is your adorable, witty, gay, charming, insouciant, spendthrifty, happy-go-lucky *self*—Hoki-Sama—Sans Souci, Soy-saucy, Slap-happy, Sing a while, stay a while. Tokuda of the Tokugawa period.

Your ever faithful, tender, loving
devoted fool of a husband
Henry-San

/\\/.\\/.\\/.\\/.\\/.\\/.\\/\

(To Japan, second trip)

April 13, 1968

Dear Hoki-San

This morning comes the first letter from you since the note you gave to George. And I had just written you a long letter—very important—addressed to Tomoko. Please get it right away as it con-

74

cerns the income tax. I have now told Mr. Silverman to send the papers you are to sign to this new address—Hotel New Japan, which I take it is the *apartment* you say you have taken.

I realize now how busy you are—it must be exciting. I also realize now that the opening must have been a success, that 800 people came and not 80, as Kubo said. If they have to pay a dollar admission to enter the gallery, the gallery must do very well even without selling pictures, no? I'm truly surprised that Mr. Jin raised the prices of the paintings; I hope he knows what he's doing. As you see, they could never get such prices in Paris, nor here in L.A., and probably not in New York. Japanese people must have lots of money to spend for art. (I don't understand it, considering how little they earn, do you?)

It touched me to read of your making a speech at the gallery opening. Arigato gozaimus,* Hoki-San! And then the TV appearances and the interviews—you are doing much better than I could have done myself, I am sure. I also had to smile when you say you are confused, dizzy, lost, feel like a country girl, and all that. Really! (maybe you are getting rusty, living the easy life in Los Angeles!)

You say you stayed two days in Shizuoka—that means with your parents, I suppose. How was your brother—the "anarchist"! I am very much interested in him. He sounds like the most interesting member of the family, aside from yourself. I read the other day about how they demonstrated against the American hospital in Tokyo. Good for them, Banzai! If the Japanese are really smart, really farsighted, they will cooperate more and more with Red China, and not U.S. and Germany. We are going to be pushed out of Asia before very long. I listened to a wonderful retired American General the other day, who knows all Asia well and served in Vietnam, and he says the *South* Vietnamese hate us more than they do the Viet Cong. And I can believe it. You speak of watching the news on TV, the riots in Washington—plus 84 other cities. L.A. was the only city in which there has been no trouble. (A miracle) But there will be more trouble soon again. The Negroes are not going to follow Dr. King's policy of non-violence, they are going to fight harder and harder. They can cause so much trouble, if they really put their minds to it, that we will have to call our soldiers back from Vietnam to stop the riots here. (Tell your brother that.)

My letter of yesterday may have sounded very businesslike. I had so many things to tell you and besides that I was a bit peeved not hearing from you in all this time. You ask if I miss you just a little. Yes and no. Yes, to be honest. No, because I see so little of you when you are here that there isn't much difference. Since you left my attacks of insomnia, due to my itching toe, began again. I guess my toe reacts to your absence. Though I pretend to myself that it makes no difference whether you are here or in Tokyo, my toe tells me otherwise. Sometimes I feel that I am married to two women, without benefit of either. One does the washing for me and the other gives me a massage now and then. Between times they are running around like chickens with their heads chopped off.

Well, to change the tune . . . So the meals are wonderful there. Good! Maybe when you return you or Puko (my massage wife) will make me some good Japanese meals occasionally, eh? I could use them. I get tired of Sue's cooking for myself two or three times a week—and my meals taste good to me. All I need now is my third wife, my fucking wife! Maybe you can bring one back for me from Tokyo?? The last line of your letter says you'll be thinking about me every minute, ha ha! But when will you get time for that?

I had several letters from Larry, who keeps talking about your making some music for him as promised. Will tell you more about that in next letter. It seems he has talked to his agent about recordings and is quite serious about all this. Do you honestly believe you could do something, with or without me—I mean, without my writing words for you? Last night, I got out Tony's drum and, during the commercials, I practiced quite a bit. Not bad. Then I did a little false piano technique. Quite good I thought. I guess what pleases me is simply to be able to manipulate my fingers, no matter what wrong notes I strike. As a gag I'd like to do a recording of this kind of piano work—some people might be fooled into thinking it was "far out new music", what!

MARRIAGE

You didn't say in your letter how many paintings have been sold thus far. At the prices you mention I'd be surprised if a dozen had been sold. (I still can't believe that 30 were sold before the show opened.)

Have you had a chance to speak to Tomoko about a possible film of "The Smile" or about the documentary film? Regarding the latter, everything is now at a standstill until some money is raised. Bob has about nine hours of film and the same for dialogue. But to edit it, synchronize it and all the other things he needs a lot of money. Letters to potential investors are going out now. We'll see what happens.

You say you'll be at this address for a month. What then? Do you expect to return home then, or what? As far as the Income Tax is concerned it won't matter when, because as I wrote you in my letter of yesterday Mr. Silverman will be sending you three sheets to which to sign your name, and that's all that will be necessary. Do let me know soon as possible whether you get this letter and the one of yesterday, won't you please. My best to Puko, Tomoko, your father and brother. I must stop now. I'm very hungry. Have been in the pool—just wonderful. Write as often as you can. I'm like Tony now—I need letters. Don't overlook any of your old sweethearts. Turn night into day, have fun, and stay chaste, like a good Japanese wife, yes-no, ha ha, ho ho! Did you get your passport changed to your new name? Nam myoho renge kyo! On my tombstone I want you to have inscribed: "The tigers of wrath are wiser than the horses of instruction." Cheerio now and Dewa Mata.

Your lonesome
Henry-San
(Husband who loves you very much!)

* Thank you very much.

/\.\/\.\/\.\/\.\/\.\/\.\/\.\

Dear Hoki-San,

Hope by now you received my two letters of recent date. No further word from you meanwhile. (We have been hunting everywhere for the iron—to iron clothes—guess you took it with you, eh?)

Had a strange letter the other day from a young (21 yr. old) Japanese married woman, offering to sell me very rare erotic books and original prints by Hokushi and Utamaro—all for $5000.00. I told her I don't have that kind of money, but suggested she try Kubo or Jin. If they were what she said they were they might be worth more than $5000.00. I only mention it because she said she left something for you to see at the Hotel Otani, but when she returned you were no longer there. Her name is Machiko Ipposhi, from Oyama City, Tochigi-ken. She enclosed a pen and ink copy she made herself of one of the erotic prints (Utamaro's I think.) Very erotic—a penis like a carrot—and the position as usual in Japanese prints—I mean, only could be done by acrobats who are double jointed.

Riko was over to make me a wonderful meal. I'm going to opening of her show Saturday night—something by Kienholz, who caused a scandal at the County Museum a year ago. Maybe the police will be there!

Am going to eat at Gerald's tonight, with Joe Gray, who just got back from Mexico. Then we go to see Bonnie and Clyde.

Tony is now at Fort Sam Houston in San Antoine, Texas, but I don't have his mail address yet. He'll be back toward end of June for a 30 day leave, but hopes to fly home now and then for a weekend. I spoke to him on the phone as he was leaving for Texas.

Jules Dassin is calling me tomorrow, about the "Cancer" film. Expect to see him here. Has Tomoko talked to anyone yet about

"The Smile" or the documentary film? Did you get a good price for your mink stole?

I was made a "Knight" of "The Order of Mark Twain"—by Mark Twain's grandson. This is the third time I have been made a knight—but I forget what the other two were for.

Tomorrow I go with Benny, and Nonko to have dinner at George Aulds home. Hope I meet some comedians there. I keep drumming like a madman during the commercials. Must get Bob to photograph me doing this—for the documentary film.

Got a clipping about you with a lovely photo of you—looking very sombre and mysterious, like Madame X. Don't know yet what it's about.

Must stop now—have a visitor. Be good to yourself. Love all around. Took down the Japanese picture over fireplace and gave it to Riko to give away. (Because she said you hated it—too vulgar or something.) Ho ho!

Cheers!
Henry.

/\/\/\/\/\/\

April, 18, 1968

Dear Hoki-San,

Just received about 40 to 50 catalogs and more posters, large and small, from Mr. Jin. Don't know if this is in answer to my first letter to him, requesting fifty, or if you have seen him and asked for 100— and then maybe this is the first half of the shipment—or is it possible he can send only this amount?

Here is Tony's new data—he telephoned me from Texas yesterday: Pvt. H.T.M., same U.S. number as before, then this: Company B-2nd Battalion—USMED TC—Class 23S—Fort Sam Houston, San Antonio, Texas (78234). Please give to Puko.

Received another letter this morning from the young woman in Oyama City, saying she is sending me a negative of a photo which I should get developed. Haven't seen the negative yet. I wrote you yesterday about her and the offer she made me to buy certain books and prints for $5,000.00.

Last night we saw Bonnie & Clyde. It was frightfully disappointing to me. One of the worst pictures I ever saw. I didn't even smile, let alone laugh. Gerald, Diane and Joe Gray all felt the same way. I would have walked out after the first ten minutes, it was so boring. I am so furious to think that this film could win such popular approval that I am thinking to write an article about it, which I may send to some magazine, or if not, to a prominent newspaper. Let me know if it has been shown in Japan yet, please. I may want to send my article to a good Japanese magazine. If I had had a Molotov cocktail handy I would have thrown it at the screen. The theatre was crowded but silent—no laughing whatever. The only good thing was the woman Bonnie, who is a perfect sexy bitch—but with no brains.

Fortunately, after that I came home, switched on the TV and heard a wonderful conference on the famous "I Ching" or "Book of Changes", which I suppose you never heard of. And after that Joey Bishop did impersonations which were out of this world—it was an anniversary program for his first year on TV. That took the bad taste out of my mouth. But when I woke up this morning I was still furious about Bonnie & Clyde and every one connected with it.

That's all for now as I am going out with Benny and Monko in a few minutes.

Cheers!
Henry-San

MARRIAGE

/\\/\\/\\/\\/\\/\\/\\
.·.·.·.·.·.·.·.

April 22, 1968 (Monday)

Dear Hoki-San,

Your letter came quick—two days early. You will get mail from Silverman any day now. So if you move from your present hotel, do let me know in advance by a few days, so that letters won't go astray. The income tax you are to sign is very important; soon as you do it I too will sign and that means I will get my refund money (quite a sum) more quickly. And I need money; I am still waiting to get my annual royalty payments from my big publishers—maybe next month.

Now, about Kawade and Kubo . . . We made it absolutely clear to Kawade about two weeks ago, after receiving check from them, that they are to pay us for the two small *original* water colors which I signed for Mr. Kawade (and which they made lithographs of)— $200 for each one. You say I "dedicated" them to Kawade. If you mean I signed my name on them "For Mr. Kawade", yes. But I did not give them to him as a gift. They paid for everything except $300.00, which they are to give me when I sign the lithographs. I am waiting for Mr. Kubo to send me his lithographs to sign. It was very nice of him to pay you in yen $1,000.00. That is what he promised me for the lithograph; in addition he is to pay me $400.00 for the two small original water colors which he wanted. Nothing more, if I remember rightly. Please make this clear to him. And don't spend the yen he gave you, please. Can't you get dollars for yen over there and send me a check on an American bank, or through the American Express Co.? I'm sure there is a way to do this. My Japanese publishers send Hoffman in Paris checks in francs—I am sure one can do the same with dollars.

I am pleased and surprised about the number of people who came to see the Tokyo show, and who paid admission to get in—represents quite a little sum. But I don't think the number of paintings sold is in proportion to the number of visitors. It is very much like

Paris again—big crowds but small sales. And I don't understand why the gallery raised the price by 20% in addition to Mr. Jin's raising the price by $200.00 on each category of paintings. It seems to me they cut their own throats in doing this. Now you say they will lower the price in other cities. Well, I suppose that is very Japanese, but it's a funny way to do business. A little too clever, too eager, too hungry.

As for the etchings . . . Yes, the price could be lowered to $150.00 or to $125.00 per etching, if Mr. Jin wishes. However, it is true that there are only these few left—what he has, and they will be worth a lot more money in a few years, because no more prints can be made of them. I don't believe there were more than 50 or 75 made of each of these etchings; you can't turn out etchings as you do lithographs: the plate from which they are printed won't permit a great many to be made. My plates (which are in Berlin) can not be used to make more etchings now. So, let Mr. Jin use his own good judgment about what price to sell them for. (If he can't sell them there I can here, or in Sweden, where I am having another show in another city there by the same man who gave the first show, in Uppsala. He wants all the paintings of mine he can get. But he is getting them from the Westwood Art Assoc., to whom I donated many paintings.)

(To come back to the 20% increase in price by Isetan Gallery. They are charging Mr. Jin 20% for use of their gallery. If they now added 20% to the price of the paintings, that means that they are making 40% and not 20% as originally figured. Right?)

From your letter I take it that you have already been to Kyushu and are now (probably) in Osaka. You mention going to Fukuoka City for one day (yesterday)—I suppose that is in Kyushu, yes? And are you now back in Tokyo again? Are you going to other cities too or what? I wait for your next letter which you say you are writing today, the 22nd. ??? You haven't written me much, to tell the truth, considering the tons of letters I saw you dispatch when you were in Europe, not to speak of all you write when here. Your English is quite good, and even if you make mistakes it doesn't bother me. I would rather have lots of letters with mistakes than a few letters perfectly written. I can't believe that you are kept so busy working for me and Mr. Jin that you don't have time to write.

The Jaguar has been fixed as much as possible, except for the radiator grill, which is very difficult to straighten out because of the metal used. And the door still has a big scratch on it. The underpart of the car was badly bent but has been fixed. So far it has cost $190.00. You must have had a bad accident—or whoever was driving it. Incidentally, Kobuko had a slight accident driving her Volkswagen; nothing serious—just bruised her knee and her chin. She feels confident she will pass her driving test—but the floor shift bothers her. I saw her a couple of nights ago. She didn't know where you were. (Which reminds me that I only received the card you wrote on the plane two days ago!!) Remember, please, if there is anything you write that is important, or if you send me a check, be sure to send it *registered* mail.

Val is coming here in a week or so, with a girl friend, to stay a week or ten days. I will give her Tony's room. Tony did not get a few day's leave, as he expected, but was sent directly to Fort Sam Houston, Texas, where he will be until June 21st or June 27th, with no permission to fly home between times. Joe Gray has a great friend in San Antonio who knows all the big politicians *and* the generals in the Fort, and he will try to get them to keep Tony in America instead of being sent to Vietnam. In giving you Tony's present address there I may have left out one thing—here it is: After "Class 238" write "Bld. 1231." (For Puko) Tony telephoned me from Texas saying it was much better there and much easier; he gets off at night and can then wear civilian clothes. Seemed much happier.

So—what else? Oh yes, last night I sat up till three in the morning watching a long film (1961) called "A Majority of One", with Alec Guinness and Rosalind Russell. It was about a Jewish widow and a Japanese millionaire—beautiful love affair. I enjoyed it very very much and was amazed at how well Rosalind Russell played her Jewish role. In fact, I'm writing her a letter to congratulate her on her fine performance. I liked Alec Guinness too, the way he impersonated a rich Japanese business man, but I am not qualified to judge if it was a good interpretation or not. The theme, of course, was an impossible one—but it was beautifully acted out. I am waiting to hear from you as to whether Bonnie & Clyde has been showing in Japan or if it is still to come, because I am still furious about this film and would love to let the Japanese know what I, as an American, think of it. I detest Warren Beatty, who played Clyde—only I am sorry that he is Shirley MacLaine's brother. Maybe he is only a half-brother??? He seems like another species entirely.

I had a strange letter from Mr. Koga, that young man whom you despise so much and who you said didn't even know his own language. He said he would never again "invade my privacy". I can only interpret that to mean that he must have tried to contact you and was turned down—or something like that. Mr. Ueno, on the other hand, said he would not presume to appear in Tokyo or to approach you, disturb you, but hopes to see the show when it comes to some city near him—he's in Ichinoseki, if you remember.

Ah yes, and that young woman from Oyama City has written again, this time in Japanese, because she said she heard that I have a Japanese teacher named Funiko. I am waiting for Michiyo to translate it for me. She sent a roll of film which I am also getting developed; they are probably photos of the erotic prints she hopes I will buy. She thinks I am "a sex maniac" and that I therefore would love to have these prints and pay any price for them. Of course she is mistaken, on both counts. Did she write you again, I wonder? She mentions a very special, very unusual book of erotic art—the Higa or Higo Book—do you know it?

I'm glad Mr. Jin is mailing me more catalogs. I can use them. So far he sent me about 60. Every one who sees the catalog thinks it unusual, out of this world, beautiful—et cetera. I sent one to Time and one to Life Magazine.

This afternoon the producer of my play is coming to see me. He is getting ready now to put the play on—it follows on Ray Bradbury's play, which wasn't so good, I understand. And Jules Dassin I will also see soon—he had to go to Cleveland unexpectedly, that was why the delay. And now what about Tomoko and my "Smile" and the "documentary" film—any news?

What gives with Puko? You don't mention her in your letters.

MARRIAGE

This week I go to see a French film called "The Battle of Algiers" which Gerald just saw; says it has wonderful shots of Tokyo in it—beautiful shots. Last night I went to see a belly dancer (with Nany, her father and mother) in an Arab joint called "Fez", Vermont near Sunset—maybe you know it. First we had dinner in a Hindu restaurant, also on Vermont. Very interesting small, quiet place—the Taj Mahal.

Attended Koko's opening for Kienholz exhibition Saturday. Good crowd but don't believe any sale will be made. I liked Kienholz himself very much—but work was not too good, I thought. Tonight, here at house, we see a short documentary on Big Sur which two friends of mine from up there made. They would like to do one based on my book—"Big Sur and the Oranges of Hieronymus Bosch". They are "fairies". But nice ones. I have to think it over. I still wish and hope and pray that some Japanese film company would do one of my books. And that's that for to-day—OOF! My visitor comes in ten minutes. So long, stay good, write more, say something personal, something meaningful, something from the heart—*if you can.*

Henry-San

P.S. Steve is coming to Japan soon—to stay six months on job there. I gave him your address. Also, my friend Bill Webb and his wife will look you up—they arrived a day or so ago.

/\.\/\.\/\.\/\.\/\

April 23, 1968

Dear Hoki-San-Sama-Sensei-Secretary-at-large and Omanko extraordinary, greetings!

I hope that the enclosed letter to Shinco-sha is intelligible to you. If they are really sincere they will get in touch with you. I thought it better to ask them to see you or talk to you than for you to go to them. It is all very complicated, but you are a bright mind and a noble soul, and what may seem like a jungle to me may only be a rippling pool of bright clear water to you. Let's hope so.

I wrote you a brief letter earlier today, concerning your income tax report—feel sure you must have Silverman's letter by now.

Can you tell me what *Mr. Jin is charging me for the catalogs* he is sending? I assume price (to me) must be around one dollar. If it is not two or three dollars, then please have him send me *fifty more*—that is, fifty above the 100 I asked for. They are going rapidly and in great demand. By the way, at *what price does he sell them to buyers in Japan?* Does he sell them at the show or what? Or are they given away free to those who pay admission to see the show?

It seems to me that Isetan did very well even without sale of paintings. You said they got 50 cents admission from 15,000 visitors. That's about $7,500.00. A lot of money. On top of that they get 20% on the sales, and on top of that they added another 20% to the price of the paintings, you said. Some business men! What pikers we Americans must be!

Incidentally, did you ever hear or see *Mr. Tanaka* of Kamakura? I'm just curious.

Tonight I have to help Miss T'ang make up subtitles for her Chinese film.

Yesterday I met Mr. Bushnell who is getting ready to stage my play (Harry). He is going to make a video tape of a few scenes in order to show potential investors. He only has to raise $32,000.00 to put the show on. Ray Bradbury's piece was a flop—lasted only 5 weeks—lost money on it. But he has great hopes regarding my play. He put an ad in the paper to get people for the cast of players —and got over 300 letters from actors who hope to have a part in the play. Not bad! If the audiences are as enthusiastic as the would-be actors the play will be a success. I don't think it will go on till June or July. If it's a hit, he hopes to take it to an Off-Broadway theatre. But that may be just a pipe dream.

MARRIAGE

Bob Snyder showed us a neo-Dada film (recent) by an American, also the first Dali-Bunuel film: "An Andalusian Dog." They were both lousy in my opinion. And the film on Big Sur, though rather poetic, was rather lame and tame. (Made by two fairies, which may explain why. No guts.)

Have been going, going, going all day, and still not able to sit down and write about Bonnie & Clyde—but I will. Don't forget, please, *pretty please*, to let me know if it has already been shown in Tokyo or if about to be shown. I'd like to send what I write to one of the good cultural art-literature magazines there . . . Tried to phone you at 6.00 P.M. last evening but the lines to Tokyo were all tied up. We are having a telephone strike now—that may explain why. I'm just beginning to feel normal again—had some kind of intestinal flu bug for 10 days.

All for now. Keep busy. Work your arse off, as they say. Between times tell us how you are, how you look, how you feel.

Cheers,
[Henry San]

P.S. Is Shinjaku really the "bad" district—low life—of Tokyo?

/\/\.\/\.\/\.\/\.\/\

April 26, 1968

Dear Hoki-San, the illustrious and beautiful one—Selah!

No letter from you, as promised, these last five days. Meanwhile I have written you several, and I am now getting very impatient to receive answers to my many questions.

First: have you mailed me yet the signed income tax papers sent you days ago by Silverman? Most important.

87

2. Do you know what Mr. Jin is charging me for catalogs? And have you told him to send me 50 more (over the hundred)?

3. Did he raise the price on those 19 paintings sold at Isetan by $200.00 each, plus another 20% which the gallery suggested?

4. Are Kawade and Kubo sending me soon their lithographs for my signature?

5. When will my water color album ("Dreams from Near and Far") be on sale?

6. Have you any idea how much longer you are staying on in Japan? And will you remain at the New Japan Hotel.

7. Did the hotel tell you I called twice? I called three or four times actually, but couldn't get through or else you were not there.

8. Is Puko returning with you, and is she still thinking to come in as a "maid" to work for me? This could raise some problems, as I have to inform State Bureau of any new employee, and I must pay wages, even if she doesn't accept, also I must pay State withholding tax on her salary—rather complicated. Could she find some one else to accept this responsibility?

9. Is there any remote possibility of Tomoko finding producer for either "The Smile" or the documentary film?

10. Will you let me know soon as you hear from Shincho-sha regarding letter I sent them, of which I sent you a copy?

Today you got a check for $65.00 from the Unemployment Bureau. Should I deposit it in your bank at Security First or what? You got bank statement too, showing $161.00 balance. Connie wrote you yesterday about your bill from Auto Insurance co. Do you want to send me a check for that from your Security First account or what?

I have never had a busier week than this one. Feel as if I am sitting on pins and needles. Last night I went through *80* pages of dialogue for the Chinese girl's film and helped her write sub-titles in English.

Today Omarr called to say a millionairess is interested in helping Bob Snyder get investors for the documentary film. We are to have dinner with her Tuesday evening. She's rather homely, fortyish, and hungry for a man. If only I can persuade Bob to give her a lay we might have some luck.

The man who published "Order & Chaos" (that beautiful book) is now eager to do "The Insomnia Series", a deluxe, extra beautiful job. I am going to begin writing text for it next week. It's going to be a crazy text, that's for sure.

Night before last went to dinner at Gimpels. Very wonderful evening. Zubin Mehta was there and this time we hit it off marvelously. I got him to let his hair down and become a human being. It worked like a charm . . . Could tell you lots more but have no time now. Alors, dewa mata from your Dai Sensei and forlorn husband.

Henry-San

P.S. Some one sent me clipping from Japan of interview with you. (You had a dark, mysterious look—beautiful!) *But*, translation says "You don't miss me. . . ."

$$\wedge\!\!\wedge\!\!\wedge\!\!\wedge\!\!\wedge$$

April 27th '68 (Midnight)

Dear Hoki-San, descendant of the Samurai—what ho?

No letter from you yet. Beginning to wonder if my letters are going astray. Sent last one, yesterday, *special delivery*. I forgot one question in my last letter. No 11—Are you thinking to have *that operation* you talked about? If you are, be sure to inquire first if it will make you more masculine than you already are. On the other hand, if you do have operation, it may alter your attitude about sex —for the better.

Joe Gray asked me to tell you that if it were no great inconvenience, and if you had the money to lay out for it, please bring him a small camera with a "built-in" meter, meaning you don't have to adjust for distance. Something around $35 or $50.

Saw the "Peace" riots on TV (in Tokyo) today. Those Geukurea (?) students are great. But your police are even more vicious than ours, I feel. I hope your brother didn't get hurt. (Did you give him the typewriter?)

I'm surprised you gave Mr. Jin two of the water colors to sell. I thought *you* were going to sell them to you friends. (Did you give your father his?)

Am trying to break the bad habit of going to bed late and getting up late. I have so very much to do—I can't afford to sleep till noon every day. Today I received a Japanese magazine with about five pages of pictures from the exhibition. There was one of you and Puko looking at each other in the gallery. Jin says he is sending me reviews and photos. I am very curious to *read what the critics have to say.*

If I don't get a letter from you by Monday morning I'm going to stop writing to you. I can't keep on writing to a stone wall. You're wrong if you now think I'm used to this silent treatment. It not only exasperates me but it also makes me wonder if you have any feeling about me other than that of being a convenience. I wonder what your interviewers would think if you were to give them a true picture of our daily life together—or apart, rather? From what I've read you make it sound like a bed of roses. But is it? Did it ever occur to you that I may not have gone to Japan for different reasons than I gave you? I'll let you try and guess. I told you once, and I meant it, that you have some truly noble qualities. But you have also some very childish, very selfish traits. They don't sit well together. You shouldn't push your luck, as we say. Or, in poker parlance, don't overplay your hand. Patience is something to be appreciated, not abused. I am beginning to lose patience. It's up to you to restore it. I don't have to tell you how. And that's it for tonight.

Your
Henry-San

MARRIAGE

/\\.\/\\.\/\\.\/\\.\/\\.\/\\.\

Dear Hoki-San, Queen of the Azores and darling of Shizuoka,

Bon Jour! Just got your letter of the 26th mailed from Shizuoka. At last! Yesterday I sent you another special delivery letter to Hotel New Japan—all letters sent there except first one care of Tomoko. You must have written yours on the 25th or the 24th possibly. Now I find that Silverman only mailed you the papers on the 22nd—and so, by now you should have them, if you are back in Tokyo. I do hope this catches you before you leave for Osaka. And *after Osaka what*? Do you return to Hotel New Japan for couple more weeks or what?

I was very happy to get this letter from you and especially for the last line—"I miss you". That is what I have been waiting to hear. I hope it's true. I will try telephoning again, to Hotel New Japan. You say they will find you even if you are somewhere else, right? I hope so. I could phone you to your father's home too, if I thought you were still there resting up.

Thank you for telling me where the iron is and about Tony's things. You seem to be answering letter of weeks ago. I have written five or six times, at least, since I enquired about those things. Wondering if you get them all?

Reading about your expenses I realize you need more money. I suppose you are using the money Mr. Kubo gave you, yes? That would be the simplest way. You used to be angry with me when I told you how expensive Tokyo was. You laughed at me and said you knew your Tokyo and how to live there cheaply. *But now you see differently.* I'm surprised that neither Kawade or Shincho-sha offered to pay any of your expenses. I wrote you about Shincho-sha —sent you copy of my letter to them. Did they ever contact you?

The special delivery letter which I mailed you last night had a little spice in it which you may not like. I couldn't help it. Every

91

day and sometimes during the night I look for letters from you, but none come. I say to myself—she can't be *that* busy working for me! She's just running around, having a good time and doesn't care whether she writes or not—she knows Henry-San is patient. Now you ask whether I'd prefer a long letter or more short ones. (Ha ha!) I want both! Or let's say I would *like* both. What I'd like and what I get are two different things. So I leave it to you. Let me see what your heart dictates. Anyway, I am sorry to have said some of the things I did in this last letter.

My dear Hoki, it's nice of you to tell me you will take care of me some day. You know, I don't expect that of you, unless I become a hopeless invalid. I talk about money because I don't seem to be earning what I used to, and money that is due me is very slow in coming in. Every day I have to think about money, how to get it, whom to write to for it, and so on. It drives me nuts. I hate to think about money. Lately, some money has come in from book royalties, but a lot more is due me. However, if I get that refund from the Income Tax people, and if the show in Japan is really a success, everything will be O.K. I don't expect to make much money from my play—theatre productions never bring much unless it's a Broadway hit. Anyhow, the show won't go on until June or July. I haven't yet heard from Jules Dassin, but I know I will any day now. A last word about money . . . Those who have money always say—it's not what you earn, it's what you save! One can earn a fortune and throw it away foolishly. I threw away over a hundred thousand dollars, as I told you before, helping people whom I thought needed it and would repay me. I will never get this money back, I see now. People borrow easily but forget to repay. My nature is such that I hate to say No! but I'm beginning to learn how now. Incidentally, I am hoping to *find some woman who would come everyday,* cook at least the dinner, and clean the house and do the laundry. People tell me I should be able to get some one to do that for maybe $50.00 per week (!) But they mean some one who will live in the house, and I don't want that. But even if I paid more, it would still be cheaper than what I'm paying now—for cleaning, for *laundry, for Sue.* So I am looking around.

MARRIAGE

I am very pleased to hear you may do a part in a film. And how nice of you to say you want it to be shown in America—so that I may see you act. Yes, I would love that! And then the 14 songs for the L.P. Sounds great. As for writing a song for you, I will try, but I can't promise. It is something new to me and I am not sure I have the talent. Incidentally, I never sent you Durrell's letters about the recordings. He seems very serious and he has a good agent. Also recently I met a young man who works for Liberty Records here; he wants me to make some talking records. I think I could persuade him to make some of your singing too. I met him through George Auld, Benny's friend, the saxophone player, remember?

I will certainly be on the alert for Mr. Okuda. I will have him meet Bob Snyder and see what he can do about the documentary film. Sounds interesting. Tomorrow night we have dinner with that millionairess who may help put up money for the documentary.

Another thing . . . The Loujon Press in Arizona, who did the beautiful book on Hans Heichel, is serious about publishing "The Insomnia Series". He wants to do an extraordinary job—even better than the Heichel book. Is now trying to find someone to finance it. I will soon start to write the text to go with these water colors. This is where Hoki Tokuda, the siren of Imperial Gardens and Chinatown comes in. If I don't succeed in writing a song for you I will certainly write a text about you . . . In one way or another you will be famous in the next few years—before you are forty!

I told you that I wrote that crazy girl with the erotic books that I was not interested. She has written again, sending photos of some of the prints (but very bad photos). But I am not answering and had no intention to do so. But if you have anything of hers be sure to return it or she could cause trouble. She is hungry for money, it seems.

One last thing . . . I explained to you about Kawade. *I am still waiting to receive their lithos which I am to sign.* Why couldn't you give them to Mr. Okuda also? I hope you made everything clear to Mr. Kubo. I would never dream of mistreating him . . . Well, that's about all for today. I will try telephoning again. Write a little or write a lot, *but write!* When we want to say, In English, I miss you very much, we say—"I miss you like sin." That's how I miss *you*. Let me know roughly when you think you will be coming back.

Your Henry-San

P.S. I met twice again recently with Mr. Kaper, the man who composes music for the films. I think you met him once at Dr. Sheinkoff's. He is a wonderful man, and I am going to invite him for dinner and ping pong (he's a good player) soon. He might be a good help in writing music for songs—and how to get them published. He has written a number of hits himself. He is an old friend of Mr. Gimpel. This is just a thought.

I'll try to write words for a song, yes.

We are busy, busy, busy, every day. Fortunately, I'm not a night owl (like you) also!

Take good care of yourself. Don't come back worn out. Jin sent me a color picture of the gallery. It's absolutely fantastic. You look so small and fragile—like a little rose in a garden of weeds. I'm glad I wasn't there to cut the tape and make a speech. They all look so serious!

Give my best to your brother. Hurrah for the *Zengakuren* (?) or whatever they call themselves. The police with their big shields look like Babylonian warriors. Fantastic. Down with the police! "We want Okinawa!" *Banzai!*

/\.\/\.\/\.\/\.\/\.\

May 3, 1968

Dear Hoki San, Santa Maria, Santissima—Hai! Just got the papers for Silverman—thank you. Only two days always for your mail to come from Tokyo. Quicker than from France or Italy, or anywhere abroad. . . . So, Japanese like "Bonnie & Clyde"—too bad. I still haven't had time to write the article about this film that I want to write. Soon. Will send copy to you to place with Japanese mag or newspaper, if you like. I'm afraid to see it a second time for fear I may find something good in it.

Val and a girl friend from Aspen just arrived, to stay a few days. Riko is making dinner for us to night. Tony has had a bit of good luck, thanks to Joe Gray, who knew an important man in San Antonio. He is doing clerical work now, and safe for at least five months, maybe longer. He always asks about Puko. She should send him a good photo of herself—he would love that. I hope he's not falling in love with her—would be bad for him, since he's so young and not a potential husband. If they have good sex life together, fine. I don't want her to break his heart, you know what I mean?

I am enclosing a letter I just received from another Japanese girl. Maybe you could get in touch with her; I don't want to write to her since she is working for Mr. Jin, as you see. She sent two photos of herself—rather goodlooking, I think. Tall girl. Do what you think best. But I don't want to "sponsor" her.

Mr. Okuda has not telephoned yet. I am thinking of what you wrote—do I have any book for Japanese film producer? Am listing a number of things which might be suitable. Mostly "fragments" of books, rather than a whole book. For movies, sometimes short text is better than long book, right? The French and the Danes are interested in having the rights (for film) to "Quiet Days in Clichy" (published in Japanese by Shinryu-sha, not Shincho-sha.) Have you ever read it? I am not agreeing to anything yet because they want to make erotic parts sensational, very daring, shocking, etc. But there is one section of this book which could make a good film, I think—it is about a prostitute named Mara-Marignan. Read it and see—and if you agree, show it to Tomoko. Of course, it would have to be expanded, this part, but any good script writer can do that. Too bad Tomoko hasn't been able to do anything about "The Smile at Foot of Ladder." That story, I feel, would be suitable for Japanese, because it is universal, not local, and they know how to handle fantasy. I have other things to suggest—later.

Now here is one other little thing for Tomoko, if I may impose on her. My opera, based on "The Smile". Japan is reputed to have good opera, far out opera, experimental, etc. This opera is not like an Italian opera; it is dramatic, music unconventional, deriving from Bartok, Schoenberg, and such like composers. It has a ballet for the circus scene, which is the high moment; and an expanded orchestra, I believe. It has been shown with great success for over two years in (German) in Germany, and recently in Italian in Trieste, Italy, and last in French, at Marseilles. All received excellent reviews from the critics. The conductor of San Francisco Opera was also interested, but he wanted to make changes in the score which my friend, the composer, refused to permit. I give you now the composer's name and the name of the publisher who puts out the score. Composer and author of the libretto: Antonio Bibalo, Goen— Ostre Halsen (by Larvik) Norway. Publisher: Wilhelm Hansen Musik Forlag, Gothersgade 9-11, Copenhagen, Denmark. Person to write there is Fru Hanne Willuh Hansen, Director.

If any interest is shown I can furnish interesting account of my meeting with Bibalo in Denmark (several times), his stay in the hospital in Copenhagen, where they furnished a piano in his room, how he fell in love with a nurse and was kicked out, his early adventures as a soldier fighting for three different countries, etc. etc. etc. Long story. He has won prizes for piano pieces, concertos, etc. Now writing opera on Macbeth and has commissions for symphonies and other works. I supported him for about three years—until recently when he has become able to take care of himself. . . . I sent Mr. Jin some material about this opera; I think he still has it. Ask him.

I must tell you that I have had one piece of luck after the other ever since I began saying every day, many times a day: *Nam myoho renge kyo!* I remember you laughing at me, as if I were a bit dotty in the head, when I told you I would use this magic formula. If I remember right, you said that everybody in Japan knew this phrase, and that it meant nothing more, had no more significance than when we say "God bless you!" when somebody sneezes. Am I right? Do you think it makes a difference, perhaps, *how* one says it—I mean, if one says it in all seriousness, believing in it, and not asking for petty favors? I know you are very skeptical about all that concerns religions, you are a born doubter, and a bit of a cynic when it comes to spiritual matters. But tell me more about these words, if you will. And whether you think I am a damn fool, or senile! As you know, I do lots of things other people regard as ridiculous or superstitious. I am a born believer, and a "fool" in the best sense of the word, a fool like Parsifal, for example.

When I say the words I most often think of some one else, some one to whom I wish good luck. I say it for *you* especially, and for *you-and-me*, if you get what I mean.

I got more catalogs today from Mr. Jin—all I asked for. If later on he can spare more I will take all he can send. I still don't know what he is charging me for them; I hope not much more than a dollar a piece . . . By now you must be back in Tokyo. How was it in Osaka? Good? Did you have to make more speeches and appear on television again? I had a post card from Bill Webb who tried to see you but couldn't. He raves about Japan—says it is even more wonderful than I imagine it to be. Thinks he has a Japanese publisher for the new edition (enlarged) of "To Paint is to Love Again".

Glad Puko is holding her own with Norwegian lover. Sorry you don't want to see your crazy brother. By the way, could you tell me where to find that vibrator I gave you? I want to try it out. When you come home I'll try it on you, how's that? It makes me feel very good to read that "you think about me all the time". When I'm gone you'll miss me even more. And then it will be too late. I must stop now, if I am to do anything more today. (Now reading proof on another book of "Correspondence" between myself and an American Ambassador I knew years ago. Fascinating. I first wrote him to Addis Ababa, then to Ethiopia, later met him in Nice. He saved every letter I ever wrote him, it seems. (Like I do yours, only my collection is still rather slim.) But I believe the day is soon to come when you *will* write me long letters, lots of them, when you *will* give me long and passionate kisses, when you *will* prefer to stay home nights and not paint the town red. For some reason I believe in you with all my heart, even if I were told, as I am always being told by some idiot or other, that you are unfaithful to me.

You look wonderful in all the photos I see of you in newspapers and magazines. And I even like your new hat!

I made two attempts to write a song—but they are no good. Will keep trying. Stop. Full stop!

And God bless you!

/\\.\\/\\.\\/\\.\\/\\.\\/\\.\\/\\.\\/\\.\\

Saturday May 4th 1968

And how are you today, Mrs. Miller, Venus of the Far East? Getting the habit of writing you daily and thinking of you in my dreams.

So—the Japanese have fallen for Bonnie and Clyde! (Guess I mentioned that before.) Pass on.

Herewith a clipping about the Hippies at Big Sur. What a story! All full of syphilis—wow! To think it all began with Columbus. It was his sailors who brought syphilis to Europe after discovering America. Did you know that?

Under separate cover I am mailing you a little pamphlet about "Into the Night Life" book. Give it to someone who might write about it. I have about 45 copies left—maybe with all the publicity attendant upon the show, there may be some rich collectors in Japan who will want to buy copies. (*At $250.00 each.*)

Sorry I am always talking *business* with you. But you seem well able to combine business with pleasure and more along same lines— In your diary keep record of money you earn or take in for me. For example, make record of $1,000.00 Kubo gave you for the lithograph. I have to show this in my account to Silverman. We can't cheat or cover up—no monkey business!

MARRIAGE

By the way, is Mr. Jin going to buy any of my water colors for himself? *And*, do you think I should make him a gift of some kind for all his kindness?

About gifts . . . please don't bring any for me. I have everything I need. (Unless someone gave you an "erotic illustrated book" by one of the Japanese masters. But don't *buy* one! On second thoughts —such a book could be seized at customs here . . . Should one fall into your hands, best way would be to mail it *first class, registered mail*. Eh what?)

But I wish you would bring some useful, and esthetic gift for Diane Robitaille. Some day I will tell you the story of the first ten years of her life, which explains her manner, her behavior—silence and self-sufficiency. I went to their apartment not long ago. Looks very bare. Needs a few comforts. I'd go crazy if I had to spend my days in such a place. Later, I must try to find them a more cheerful spot—at least with a good view from the windows.

Val is cooking me a good meal for dinner. She has become quite a cook in recent months. Seems happier, more contented now. Am really glad to see her again. We talk more easily now.

I am waiting for you to come back soon. Maybe we two can also talk more easily now. I know you will have a lot to tell me about Japan—but I mean other kind of talks as well. Like "person to person", "Man to man", "husband to wife", "lover to lover"—ha ha, ho ho!

I know I am flooding you with mail. I hope you read all my letters. I don't want to spoil you—but of course, as you once told me yourself—you are already spoiled. (But don't become like America, as one Frenchman described it—"a fruit that rots before it ripens.")

I am swimming every day now—air still cool and rather foggy in the mornings—but water temperature at 86 degrees, just right for my arthritis.

Must knock off now. Hope you haven't forgotten how to speak English.

    Nam myoho renge kyo!   (For *you*!)

Love all around. Special love for you. Stay well. Keep slim. Don't exhaust yourself! And come back smiling. (Do itashi gozaimas!) Honto in arigato gozaimes!*

Your loving husband, lover and sergeant-at-arms.

Henry-San

"Playboy of the Western World"

* Thank you very very much and you're very welcome.

/\/\.\/\.\/\.\/\.\/\

Sunday—May 5th '68

Hoki-San—Light of the Orient

To my great surprise and delight, who walks in on me unannounced today but Tony! Looking fit, strong as a bull, weighing 27 pounds more, *all muscle*, and one inch taller. Only stayed an hour. But gave me lots of good news about himself. Evidently Joe Gray's friend in San Antonio has all sorts of influence. Tony may never get to Vietnam—and soon he will be promoted, etc. etc. (All because of Nam myoho renge kyo . . . which I say every day, every night.)

I gave him Puko's address (one you gave me) or to write her *care of you* at the Hotel New Japan. Suspect she is living with you. I was surprised when he said he hadn't heard from her since she left for Japan. I wish she *would* write him. He needs it, just as I need to hear from you. What went on between them I can only guess. Sex, sure. But maybe he felt more than that. A young boy like him could be far more serious than she. You know, when these kids are in the army, they dream about women all the time. That's all they can think of after their senseless drilling. So, let her be gentle with him and write! He will be back here June 21st, for two weeks, probably. Tell Puko to treat him well then—*lots of fucking* or whatever seems best. He will appreciate it.

100

MARRIAGE

Just ran across photo of girl who wanted to come to America—Miss Matsunaga. Did the Duke of Anaheim ever hire her for a maid? I haven't seen or heard of the Duke since you left. I imagine he misses you.

Sometime I'd like to explain to you *why I need your letters!!!* A long story. And I'm sure you will forget to ask me, but I mention it just the same. It's easy to do what's easy to do. The important thing is to do what is hard for one to do. There's where real character comes in. (I could tell you, for instance, what you said you would do if you married the Chinese boy for convenience. Which you never did for me. But you probably forgot what you said. I have a memory like an elephant, don't forget.)

I just wrote six pages about Bonnie and Clyde. May write more before I am finished with it. I will send you a copy—for some Japanese magazine. They may appreciate more what I say than my own Americans. We'll see.

Reading proofs today (correspondence with one of our ambassadors) I found that in 1957, at Big Sur, I had read and commented on these two books by Japanese authors. Wonder if you ever read them?

1) "Homecoming" by Jira Osaragi (pen name)

2) "Five Women Who Loved Love" by Ihara Saikaku (published in English by Tuttle and Co in 1955.) Do you think you could find it for me? Tuttle and Co. have an office in Tokyo . . .

I hear that the famous geisha—"the armless beauty", who retired to a nunnery in her late life, has just died. I read all about her in a book called "Three Geishas" by Kikou Yamata (Half French, half Swiss) with whom I used to correspond.

I should stop now, but it's hard to do. I feel I am talking to you. I talk to you (aloud) even though you are not here. I see you sitting on a big chair with nothing on but your red towel shift and your legs folded up like a jack-knife. And when I picture you thus I always think of the night Joe Gray drove you and me and Noko home to your first apartment way down town. You sat in my lap, with my hands between your legs and you let me kiss you and fondle you. Do you remember that ride?

Some time you should really tell me, write me, of some tender little thing you remember—even if "sentimental"—I would appreciate it. You can't imagine what a thrill it gives me to see "I miss you" or "I think about you all the time." You have nothing to lose and lots to gain. I want to be close to you, feel that you are my wife, that our living together means something. Don't let me dry up from lack of affection. And don't let me do anything I want with other women. Be a little jealous! It would make me happier.

Enough now. I wait to hear from you. Come home soon, if you can, yes?

Your
Henry-San

/\.\/\.\/\.\/\.\

Tuesday, May 7th

Dear Hoki-San, Pearl of the Orient, Light of Asia—Good morning and how are you today?

You sounded far away on the telephone last night, and weak as a cat—maybe I woke you up too early. By my reckoning it was one o'clock, but we are on daylight saving time now and so it may have been only twelve noon. . . . This morning I received your letter written on the train.

I'll be happy to make a special water color for Akira-San. I had written you in my last to ask if it would not be nice now for me to make him some kind of gift. You say I should put some "nice words" on the painting. I am not sure if you really mean nice, or if you mean something "pornographic"??? Please tell me. I notice that the painting I gave Fujishima, with the writing on it, appears in nearly all the mags (and the Catalog) I receive. There was a good 4-page spread in Asahi-Graphic, which it says was written by you *and*

In April, Henry sent Hoki five postcards of his own watercolors. The text which Miller wrote accompanying the postcards appears on the pages listed next to the title of each card.

ONE FISH *(page 5)*

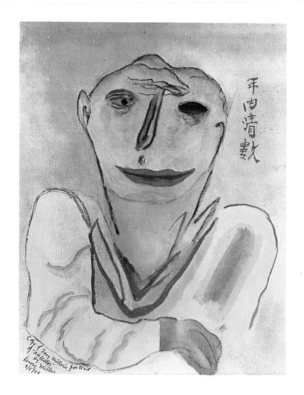

THE ANCESTOR *(page 5)*

THE HAT AND THE MAN
(page 5)

(COLLECTION OF LEON SHAMROY)

DEUX JEUNES FILLES *(page 6)*

REALLY THE BLUES *(page 6)*

MARINE FANTASY

NORTH AFRICAN

GIRL WITH BIRD *(page 27)*

Henry's present to Hoki, where, at her request, the "chin-chins" at the bottom left of painting were covered by postage stamps.

Henry's birthday painting for Hoki, to celebrate "her first birthday under the stars and stripes."

Thursday midnight

Good morning, dear
night owl, and how is
your butterfly to-day?
I thought I would
let you put this in
the waste basket for
me, along with your
unwritten thoughts.
This is a sheet of paper
on which I tested my
colors. I didn't have the
heart to throw it away
myself. Maybe you
have a little private
cemetery in which to
bury spots of color,
old love letters, broken
feathers and other such
trifles. If not, I will
make one ǂ for you.
Call at any hour of the
day or night — always
at your service. We
also repair broken skulls
and revive old skeletons.

Remember, the left hand is the dreamer.
All dreams must be played in the key
of C sharp minor!

Henry Valentine Miller
11/24/66

A note to Hoki later made into postcards and posters.

MARRIAGE

Fujishima. Had some strange things in it. I notice you frequently make mention of Durrell, what a big impression his "poetic" writing made on you. I can hardly believe his writing was well translated into Japanese, because it is difficult reading even in English. (They'll never be able to properly translate his new book, "Tunc," which the critics here claim is overdone, too much beautiful language and not enough meaning or substance.) You mention meeting Japanese writers. Even Yoshiyuki, I understand, was unable to translate some phrases of mine—from the book "Nights of Love and Laughter", which is written in fairly simple English. One of my smaller books, but one I like very much, you should try to read in Japanese; it's called "The Time of the Assassins", and is about the poet Rimbaud, the genius who wrote all his work between ages of 16 and 19(!) His life is fascinating, or was. He influenced all the great writers of France—and other countries. Died year I was born—1891. (Together with Nietzsche, Walt Whitman and Van Gogh.)

I'm not so surprised the Japanese like small water colors—the great water colorists seldom did big water colors, even in the Western world. (I think of Turner, John Marin, Paul Klee, et alia.) I guess now my paintings will sell more slowly, not like in Tokyo. If there are some left over, which you can't sell to your friends, I can donate them to the Westwood Art Assoc., which means tax reduction for me, and is just as good in a way as sales.

I was certainly surprised to hear some magazine wanted you to write an interview with Sukarno's Japanese wife. That's amazing. I wouldn't let you do an interview with Sukarno himself, because he's a great "lady killer", and you might never come home again. Durrell is now traveling in Greece, in connection with that documentary film on Katsimbalis, "the *Colossus* of Maroussi". It must be difficult now to find a room in Paris, now that the peace talks are scheduled to be held there. Do you remember that the Vietnamese Embassy was on the corner where we lived—rue d'Assas? Already there are riots in Paris, against the Americans, and the police are using tear gas, which they never did before! What paper is it that wanted you to take this commission? I'm curious.

Some one told me there is a good article about the Tokyo show in the May issue of Geijutsu Shincho (Shincho-sha's art mag.) Hope you can send me a copy. Nothing I have read so far seems really serious . . . Your Jaguar is getting a tune up now, so that it will be in first class condition when you arrive. You should remember to get the oil changed and give it a "lube" job every thousand miles—that will keep your car in condition. It looks pretty good to me now and it runs well. Connie is looking after it.

I'm adding some more pages on Bonnie & Clyde today. I made heavy corrections in my first draft, and when I send you the finished text I will also send you the corrected first draft. If you send it to a literary magazine, they may appreciate seeing the corrected pages— sometimes they like to photograph a page or two to show the reader how a writer slaves over his manuscript. I am also sending you, separately, the little pamphlet called "Journey to an Antique Land," which some magazine might like. It's a text I wrote for that crazy artist in Big Sur who makes tiny little drawings and thinks they are masterpieces.

No word from Okuda yet nor from Jules Dassin. That's because Saturn always causes delays—ho ho!

Waiting for your next letter. Hope you have a good session with Mumata. I'd like to know what you think of him, as a person. As for Kawade, what I am most eager to know is when are they going to send me the lithographs to sign. If the ordinary edition of my W.C. album is out, do mail me a copy quick—air mail! I'm dying to see it. They call it "Dreams from Near and Far", which you said you didn't think would translate very well into Japanese, remember?

Great night here last night, showing more documentary film to librarians who are interested. Played ping pong like a demon, after drinking Chartreuse and Scotch. Wasn't drunk, just gay and reckless and laughing like a fool. . . . Hope you get my letters—seem to be sending one or more every day since a week or so ago. Sorry to keep you busy with all my questions and demands. But I do appreciate the way you get things done. You're a real ambassador from PacPal. What you call a "plenipotentiary".

Coda: How very nice, how lovely, to see at last the word "love" over your signature. How wonderful it will be to see you in person soon again. I feel I could devour you.

Now for a spot of lunch—4.00 P.M. and back to Bonnie & Clyde. The last bit will be a "cadenza" to a "toccata for half-wits". My drumming is improving. Wouldn't it be funny if I end up my career not as a writer or painter but as a drummer!

Cheers now and love all around
Henry-San

P.S. Your father sent me a nice card thanking me for the water color you gave him.

P.P.S. When Val saw photo of you in Tokyo mag first thing she said was—"Where is her wedding ring?" I said, "What wedding ring?" She said, "The one from Israel." I said you probably threw it away. She sent you her love when she heard me telephoning you. I think she likes you more and more.

/\/\/\/\/\/\

May 9th, 1968

Dear Hoki-San,

A quick one today. No letter yet since the one from the speed train. About the MS. enclosed—sending you the first carbon, which is readable, because the original pages I want to send to an American mag—either Esquire, Playboy or Evergreen. Am sending xerox copies to a half dozen other foreign countries; each one will have the right to use this text only in their language and their country. As I wrote yesterday, I also send you the corrected pages; these I want back, unless some one over there wants to buy them. I can always donate pages to libraries or sell to collectors. Magazine has right to make photos and reproduce with my text, if they wish.

Some of my words and phrases are slangy; but I think a man

like Yoshiyuki can dig most of it—and if not, they can always ask me for meaning. (Some of these you may not quite understand yourself, I am not sure.) Anyway, I want it printed exactly as written—no castration, no modification, as Japanese editors have done with my books. If they won't accept as is, return text to me. A reaction is beginning to set in here as regards this film—so my text is just in time. Tonight, on the Joey Bishop show, I will hear a man whose father was killed by the real Bonnie and Clyde—he has refused to see the film and told Joey he can't understand why they "glorify" such people.

Tried my hand at another song last night, but still not right. I keep on rhyming the lines, which is not necessary. Joe Gray gave me some good ideas—how to write simply. Will try again.

Your Jaguar is now in perfect shape, mechanically. Just paid another $45.00 for a tune up, which means that you got new spark plugs (why you stalled in mornings), carburetor boiled out—was thick with sludge—, new points, engine tuned up, nuts and bolts tightened underneath, and so on. From now on you should get oil changed and a lube job every 1500 miles and every 5,000 miles a tune up, like we just got. Then your car will always be in perfect condition. I kept the bill to show you what they did, the date, etc., for reference. Connie knows where to get this job done—in Venice.

Reading proof on the Correspondence (book) by our ex-ambassador (J. Rives Childs) I see that way back in the 1950's I was trying to get a free trip on the Panam Lines to fly to Japan, in return for publicity I would write for them. In one of his letters this man, after listening to my record (conversation) with Ben Grauer of the N.B.C., N. Y., said it gave him the same sort of lift as when he first saw the Buddha at Kamakura. About that same time, Mr. Takata (the pirate publisher, who sold all my paintings and never paid me) was inviting me to come and stay at his home in Kamakura (sic).

If you are now singing the 14 songs for the record album is it possible to bring home tapes of them? I would love to hear them—before September—and they may give me ideas. For Larry I think I can do crazy, Surrealistic lyrics, but for you I want to do something rather sentimental, with a touch of Japan in it. . . . That's about it, for today, O Siren of the Rising Sun. More tomorrow no doubt. Weather fair and warmer. Bad month, this, for cloudiness and fog. Write soon and often. Be good to yourself. I'm waiting to see you. As Shakespeare says: "All's well that ends well."

Henry-San

P.S. Did you ever see Catherine Deneuve, beautiful French actress who played in film "Belle de Jour" by Bunuel?

/V.\\/V.\\/V.\\\

May 10, 1968

Hoki, Venus of Samothrace, Shizuoka and Points East: Nice to get your special delivery letter this morning. You sure are moving. Glad to hear Kawade is not (yet) on the rocks.

This must be another quick one as I am going to dinner in a few minutes with the beautiful Vietnamese wife of a friend of mine, a great art critic from N.Y. and Paris. Cancelled dinner with Gia Scala and friends—too boring.

I just paid your Auto Insurance—State Farm—$100.40, as it is due tomorrow. I had written you about this weeks ago, also about the check for $65.00 which came from the Unemployment Bureau but no reply from you. Check is made out to H. Miller. Should I sign it and deposit it to your account? I'm also paying off balance of payments for the Jaguar as I hate having monthly payments to make. Don't want any more time payment plans.

So much for "business". . . .

So you may have that operation, eh? Be very careful whom you choose to do the job. Omanko is very delicate place, as you know. Get a good man for it. Let me know when you go so that I can say —Nam myoho renge kyo! (May the gods protect and bless you!)

Last night I got out some of your sheet music to see how lyrics are written. Was surprised how poor the words are, even in the so-called good hits. I notice there is a lot of rhyming. Only I have to find the third line, which doesn't rhyme. Anyway, I keep trying. I certainly do want you to sing something of mine. I thought perhaps you would write the music for it. People say the words are the most important, but I always think the tune is the most important. If you were here and would do a little improvising I might get the words easier. Another thing—you say you would translate my words. But then it will be difficult to find just the right words for the rhyme, in Japanese, won't it? Or will you be making both an English *and* a Japanese version for Sony? You're very good in Japanese, I know, so maybe this won't be such a big problem.

If I find I can write lyrics, then I will write a number of them. Why not? There's always a chance that one song may become a hit, eh what what? And especially if it is sung by Hoki-San, the nightingale of Shinju-ku!

If I have more trouble writing lyrics, I will try writing you a love letter in prose, from which I may possibly find the right lines. I have some Japanese words I would like to introduce; if you think of any you especially like, tell me. I know one never says (in Japanese) "I love you!" But we can get round that, just like Mme Nogi gets round the Omanko with her "injo", n'est ce pas?

I listened to the man whose father was killed by the real Bonnie and Clyde last night on Joey Bishop show. He looked as if he could have been the father of Bonnie, if you remember how the mother was in the film? He was very simple, genuine, touching—made a hit with the audience. Joey is very strong against Bonnie & Clyde, it would seem. Feels it's dangerous for the teen-agers who see them as "romantic". I saw the photos of the real Bonnie & Clyde. Nothing like the film stars, and especially not Bonnie!

That's all for now, my chick-a-dee. Here's a warm hug for you. Wonder what you will think of my text on B. & C., which I mailed you "registered" yesterday.

Henry-San

MARRIAGE

/\.\./\.\./\.\./\

May 11, 1968

Shibara-ku, O Kano Sama, out there in the blue, yoohoo, yoohoo!
(Still writing rhymes in my head.) Here is the first lyric I think
comes anywhere near being a "lilic". What do you make of it?)
Maybe it will sound better in Japanese than in English. In my next
attempt I will try to ring in some Japanese words or phrases.

Here are some variations of rhyme from previous failures—just
for your amusement. . . .

Midnight babes with razor blades
Stroll the Ginza like the Braves (ball team)
Bobo, Colo, Kurimoto, all are somewhat loco

(Loco means crazy or name
of weed with drug)

While playing hockey she took her Sake
Just like Lady Murasaki
The Ginza glows with noodle shops
Dishing soup to ancient fops

(fops means silly dandies)

No admission nor tuition
Just a yen for more fruition

(Yen has double meaning;
in English "yearning"
or "craving for" (candy))

A land of ghosts that never
ask to sleep or kiss
Nor beg for just an ounce of bliss

With Mister Moto and his koto
Comes Miss Injo and her banjo

Enough of this! But you see how the rhymes are rolling around in
my head all the time. . . .
About those two water colors you like so much. I remember the red

109

boat one, but not the one with the eyes and Omanko *around the neck?????* Anyway, why don't you ask Mr. Jin to put them aside for you—or mark "Sold"?

About Kawade once again . . . I do hope they got out the ordinary album, if not the de luxe one. Let me know, please.

When I told you not to call me from Japan I was thinking (foolishly) that you might be calling and I would be out. But if you make it person to person it's O.K. Would be a nice surprise for me some time. If you call around one in the afternoon your time you ought to catch me in. That would be about eight in the evening here.

By the way, did your father's friend, that rich man who wanted to give me the show, did he ever buy a painting, do you know? I wrote a nice note to Mr. Jin the other day, telling him how much I appreciate all he is doing and that I would send him soon a little water color with writing on it, special for him. I told him how much you too appreciated what he is doing. Same goes for Mr. Kubo, of course. You mention seeing ten old paintings of mine in Kubo's private collection. Did he not lend 35 of my paintings for the exhibition? I thought that was understood.

No more questions . . . Must take my swim now. Weather still on the cool side and skies overcast. Will last this way thru May I'm afraid.

Well, I'm waiting to hear more about proposed Paris trip. But want to warn you again that it is getting dangerous today in Paris, as the students are still rioting. Over 700 policemen were injured in the first riot, and it still goes on. It's all protest over the war— anti-American. And hotels will be very hard to find now. So, take care! Did you get your passport changed to Hiroko *Miller*?

Joe will probably show up today, as usual. Glad to know you will be able to bring him the camera. Kore-wa ikura desuka? Kokade Pon-O Tomemasu. Yurushito kudasai (for poor Japanese) Wa-ga tomo! (Do itashi mashite!)

> Your dipsy-doodle dandy O
> Henry-O
> *not* O'Henry! (name of poor writer)

MARRIAGE

/\.\/\.\/\.\/\.\/\.\/\.\/\.\

May 13, 1968

copy for Hoki

Dear Larry,

I had just written Hoki two days ago that you were probably in Greece by now and here comes your letter from Sommieres. But I take it you *will* be leaving soon for Greece, non? I mention it because Hoki now has a chance to go to Paris to interview the Japanese wife of Sukarno for some Japanese magazine. And I have been warning her to think twice before going to Paris now— because of the riots—five days of it now—which I think will continue all during the Peace talks. By now over a thousand police men have been injured, not to speak of the students. That's quite something, much more than occurred in any of our bloody riots in the Negro quarters. Much much more! What intrigues her, of course, is the prospect of making it back home via Beirut, Hong Kong, and those other glamorous places. She forgets that it's the season for diarrhea, water shortages, cholera, and all that. And in the back of her mind she's probably thinking that you may come up to Paris while she's there. All this supposedly toward the end of May.

Today I am once again giving her your messages about song writing. As you may have heard, she has a commission to do a dozen songs for the Sony people. She wanted one song, the "lyliks", to be done by me, which tickled me, and so, after numerous attempts I knocked out the one enclosed and sent it to her. She has to translate it into Japanese, and God knows what happens to my "poetry" then—I mean, the rhymes. But she's very clever, Hoki-San, and even if she has to give my words a new twist it may come off alright, maybe even better than the original.

Anyway, I send you this first attempt to see what you think. I would love to do more, especially if Hoki will sing them, perhaps compose the music herself. But what a fucking business it is, these

111

lyrics! I looked through a batch of songs Hoki has here, and found them so damned simple, so asinine most of the time, even Cole Porter or Rodgers and Hammerstein, or you name it. What shit! To me it seems that the music is the principal thing, but I am told no, it's the words. The ideal is to be able to do both yourself, what!

As I wrote Hoki, I think I can knock out some goofy lyrics, with play on words, crazy lines, rhyme and no rhyme, etc. Every time I see the word "love" in these songs I want to puke. Lawrence was right—"time we did away with the word love," remember? I don't much care for ballads either, especially à la Joan Baez—they put me to sleep. And Bob Dylan leaves me stone cold, though he's Number One for the teen agers. What we have to do is to reach the half-wits of all ages, all denominations, the kids who turn the radio on soon as they start the car and make it loud as possible. Even to enjoy a plain honest fuck these kids have to have the music on. It's all in the same idiom, what's worse—rolls over you like so much sewage, if you know what I mean. But we'll have a go at it. I find that certain old tunes have much more staying power than the new ones. The words seem to match the music better too.

So you're still thinking of coming over in the Spring and touring the States, are you? Not me, my lad. I've had it. What I wrote in the "Nightmare" is duck soup compared to what has to be said today about America. If ever a revolution were possible in this country, which I strongly doubt, then we are on the verge of one now. The blacks are not going to be put down, they're not going to wait indefinitely. And, it's not only the blacks—the poor white trash is just as bad off. You'll see, if ever you travel through the south. Tomorrow begins the poor people's sitdown in Washington D.C. I hope you'll be able to watch it on TV. It will be an eye-opener. It is admitted now that we have about 15,000,000 people in this country who are starving, which means not even one decent meal a day. We used to have plenty of money for guns, but even that no longer holds. We are bankrupt, physically as well as morally. The Viet Cong hold the trump card at the Peace Conference. They can go on indefinitely, but not us.

MARRIAGE

I just knocked out about nine pages on Bonnie and Clyde. A diatribe, of course. Am sending it to a dozen different countries. You'll say I'm ranting, making too much of it, but do you know, whenever I think of this bloody film I am furious, still furious. You have a wonderful, broad threshold of tolerance. Somehow violence is one of the things I can't stand. Which reminds me . . . last night, 1.00 A.M., while taking a walk around the block suddenly a car stops short beside me and two teen agers, evidently on dope, begin to bully me, threaten me, curse me. I wasn't far from the house, so I just kept walking, they following. I thought at one point they would jump out and tackle me, but fortunately they didn't. And I who talk about violence, do you know what was in my mind then? To let them follow me right to the house, let them follow in after me, and then I'd go get my razor sharp machete, which I keep handy, and cut them to ribbons. This sort of slaughter, you see, I regard as "justifiable". Afterwards I began trembling. Not because of what they might have done to me, but what I might have done to them! Beware of the peace lovers, I always say. Beware of the just man! Do you know what it is to dance with rage? That's what I do inwardly again and again. Fortunately I always wear my Buddha-like mask.

Well, enough of this . . . If you see Joey in Greece give him a good hug for me. I'm eager too to see what old Katsimbalis looks like on the screen. Oh yes, I saw David Frost on the telly recently, here in the U.S., but must say I didn't like him, not at all. Good thing we never locked horns. Give me Cassius Clay any day. Best to Marcelle, the dear trollope, and tell her her predictions seem to be doubly true. Especially for Hoki. Alors, hoki-doki and une bonne pétarade pour tout le monde.

Henry-San
alias Val or Harry
Cheers!

/\.\/\.\/\.\/\.\/\.\

May 14, 1968

Dear Hoki-Sama, Light of Asia—O haeri kudasai!

Nobuko was just here with George of the Travel Bureau who is getting her visa extended another six months. I wrote a note to the Immigration for her, saying she was visiting us and please let her stay longer. She looked beautiful, as she always does, and happy too. (George is the guy who owned an apartment near you on So. Elden.)

Connie went to Bank of Tokyo this morning and paid for the Jaguar in full. You will have to go there when you come back to get the pink slip for your car, which they wouldn't give her or me. That's the slip you need in case you sell the car.

At last I got a good translation of "Nam Myo Ho Renge Kyo". Here it is: "There is nothing so exquisite as the law of the lotus sutra." I find it beautiful. And it still works for me, like a charm.

Today I had a letter from a young woman I once brought to see you at the piano bar, Imperial Gardens. She writes: "I wish I had gotten to know your wife better, but the important thing is that she is beautiful in all respects. . . . The two of you look perfect together. Despite your ironclad power of pen inside Henry Miller lies a velvet-gentle heart. And in your wife's face is the match for your gentleness —in her words and gestures. You long ago wrote as if you knew you would find her and as if you even wrote for her. It seems only natural that she would be part of the transcendence you then were experiencing in both sorrow and joy. . . . ."

I started a water color two nights ago, for Mr. Jin, and have been interrupted five times. Hope to finish it today. I'm on the go now —dinner out for the next four nights. Tomorrow noon I have a champagne lunch with Gia Scala who kept me on the phone three-quarters of an hour (midnight) last night, telling me the story of her life.

MARRIAGE

Seems to me I had lots more to tell you but can't think of it now. Don't forget to tell me where to find the vibrator, will you.

Ogenki de Osugoshi Kudasai! (Whatever that means.)

In Italian—Ossobuco pistachio con amore.

Waiting to hear what gives. Cheerio!

Henry-San

P.S. Val and her friend are still here.

/\\.\\/.\\/.\\/.\\/.\\/.\\/.\\

May 15, 1968

Dear Hoki-San,

Enclosed you will find letter from Art Life with copy of my reply. I am mystified. Are all the exhibitions really over now? The results, as I wrote to Jin, are certainly disappointing, considering all the effort he and I went to to make it a success. I certainly don't want to let the remaining pictures go at half price to some shrewd Japanese art dealers. I can easily have another show in America, or donate them to the Westwood Art.

Today I also received a heart-breaking letter from Ueno-San, saying he had read an article by you in which you mention that one of my Japanese fans tried to creep into my favor and asked for money to build a house—and that you go on to say I am still sending this man money. This is the worst thing you could have done to any Japanese person. It is humiliating. It is true I still send him money, but that is for his little boy who is in the hospital with some serious ailment and will be there for some time yet. (Unless all this false, in which case Ueno is a scoundrel. But I don't believe this, because he has sent me receipts from the hospital for his son's treatments.) I can not make clear whether you mentioned him by name in your article—I hope not!—but in any case he feels disgraced. He is not angry with you, though he felt terribly hurt. He

115

says you wrote good things about me and that he was happy to see how well you understand me. I wish you would send me the magazine or newspaper in which this article appeared, will you please! Ueno asked me not to say anything about this, but I cannot ignore it. I know how I would feel if such a story had been written about me instead of him. You probably didn't mean to hurt him—I imagine you were trying to explain to the Japanese public all the strange demands that are made upon me by my fans and admirers.

Incidentally, my cablegram to you was sent *before* I received Ueno's letter. Perhaps you have met him by now in Sendai. Perhaps you still regard him as a nuisance and an eccentric individual, now that you have met him. But unless he is an out and out rogue, a scoundrel, a thief and a liar, I consider him a friend and intend to treat him as such. You ought to know by now that I have many strange friends and acquaintances, and some of them far worse than Ueno-San, yet I am still their friend and, if I feel so inclined, I help them though they may lie and cheat me. The thing is not so much what people do to you but what you do to them, understand? Evil doesn't touch me, because my heart is pure. During my whole life very few people have tried to cheat me or harm me, and when they did, they suffered more than I. In other words, dear Hoki-San, what I am trying to tell you is that some guardian angel always seems to look after me and protect me. That doesn't mean that I must act like a fool and not try to protect my own interests. But it does help me not to be suspicious of people or too distrustful. Enough of this . . .

Do you have the telephone number of Elaine ——————— in Santa Monica? The one who read your cards, remember? Riko doesn't have it. That's it for today. Still no letter from you. Stay well and trust in the Lord. Amen!

Henry-San

P.S. The "guardian angel" I speak of is in the blue somewhere. *You* are my "guardian angel" here below—don't forget it! The biggest problem in life is—*how* to help some one. Do you follow me?

MARRIAGE

/\\./\\./\\./\\./\\./\\

Dear Hoki-San, little rosebud among the thorns—

Cheers! So glad to hear your voice again. What a go-getter you
are! You make us all look like wet ducks! Inexhaustible energy,
clever, brains, True devotion, etc. etc. etc. . I just can't imagine
how you manage it all. Japanese run, not walk. Japanese work, not
sleep. Japanese play hard, not dream. Sydney Omarr warned *me*
last night to take it easy, not get involved with too many projects,
etc. because Saturn is crossing Aries, my ascendant and yours, too,
I believe. Saturn makes you work hard and saps your strength. Says
I could be dead by October if I don't watch out. Henry-San not
ready to die yet—will take care, if only to see a little more of his
Hoki-San. Had merry night with "Millionairess" who is not as ugly
as reputed. She's one of my very ardent fans. Cooking dinner for
me at her home next week. As for money—We ate at La Dolce Vita
—Bob, Omarr, Joe Gray, George Raft and me. This woman—Ricky
Dupont—met you at Imperial Gardens. Raved about your beauty,
your playing, your singing. Didn't know I knew you then. She told
you you ought to find a wonderful young man to marry and you
answered—"I want to marry an old man!" (She's tall and blonde.
Has Japanese friends.)

No Income papers today—maybe tomorrow. Hope the Osaka
show goes well. Osaka not such a nice city, eh? This ought to catch
you in Tokyo after your trip. I miss you more and more. Maybe
you rent good piano when you get back, yes? More soon.

Henry-San

P.S. You made a lovely mistake in one letter. You asked me to write
a *lilic* for you—instead of lyric.") My Israeli brother-in-law is called
"Lilik". Ha ha!) Give Puko a friendly little pat on the backside for
me, please.

/\.\/\.\/\.\/\.\/\.\/\.\

Dear Hoki Mysteriosa Cantabile—

No letter from you yet and I am beginning to wonder if anything has happened to you. Are you in the hospital perhaps or did you get hurt in the earthquakes? If you can't write, please send me a night cablegram, yes?

Nobuko called me yesterday to say that her visa was extended another six months; she is supposed to be visiting you and me here. Gerald is only now about to get his working permit; they turned down his first application "because he was not a college graduate", imagine that. So now he is supposed to be my nurse and attendant as I am too old and crippled to remain alone in the house. He too is supposed to be living here.

The enclosed about the writer Oë is from Evergreen Review, Grove Press. If I remember right, he is the one who wrote the Introduction for my water color album which Kawade is publishing. (Notice the comparison they make between his writing and Mishima's.) I am very very eager to know if Kawade, in spite of their bankruptcy problems, have brought out, or at least printed, the w.c. album—the ordinary edition, if not the de luxe one. It is advertised, with prices, in the catalog of my show. We had tried to get Grove Press, N. Y. to bring out this same album with an English text, and wrote Kawade so some time ago. But Grove has never answered on this, and neither has Kawade. I have written Grove again today, telling them that this might be a good time to make such an arrangement with Kawade—it might help them. If Oë's Introduction to the album needs to be translated maybe Oë could do it himself???

In my last letter, which contained letter from Jin and my reply, you will see that it looks as if my exhibitions end in Sendai. I will wait to hear from Jin before doing anything, but here is what I have been thinking to suggest to him—that he offer the remainder of the paintings to a collector—just *one* collector—and not at a reduced price, but at a higher price than what I have marked them. My thought is, as I once told you, that now is the time for a smart and clever art dealer to buy up my work. In five to ten years he is sure to make a good profit on what he buys now. And if I die before that, he is even more sure to make money. Since the Japanese are supposed to be such good business men, I think my idea has some validity. If Mr. Jin is not able to make such a transaction I am wondering if it might not be a good idea to advertise this proposal in some good Japanese newspapers. What do you think?

Here is one more thought. . . . Mr. Kubo was supposed to let me know if I could get colored lithographs of my water colors (just one or two, to begin with) made in Japan and distributed there. He never answered me about this, so yesterday we wrote him again to remind him. I offered to let him handle the distribution himself and thus make a commission on sales.

I'm curious to know if you still think you can sell any of the water colors to your friends—at the prices I put on them. I suspect Mr. Jin is not buying any for himself. Today I mailed him (air) a little water color with writing on it just for him. I think he will like it. I didn't make a photo of it because Connie didn't have her camera here. If you or he could send me a photo, or the negative, I would appreciate it.

Joe Gray was here with another request, but only if you have the time for it. He wants ten sets of those short Japanese curtains which one hangs over doorways—you had them in your old apartment—Noren, I think they are called. You don't need to bring them with you, mail them is alright. If you think he could get them in Little Tokyo for about the same price, he will do that—let us know.

Tonight we are going to see the finished version of the Chinese film which Miss T'ang made. Sub-titles in English, thanks to Henry Miller.

That book I asked you about—"Five Women who loved love"—is coming to me from Tuttle, from their office in Vermont.

Playboy asked me to rewrite the article I sent them and suggested I speak about certain well-known erotic authors, like Casanova, Aretino and Restif de la Bretonne. I had to read through about eight volumes! And then, by a miracle, I got hold of a book which I have been looking for for over 25 years—now published by the Grove Press. And this book is greater than any of the other famous ones. By greater, I mean more frank, more casual, more honest, and more Omanko, Bobo and all the other things that go to make a sex pudding. It's called "My Secret Life", author unknown. Originally it was in 12 volumes, and Grove has now brought out in one big volume for $35.00. They are giving me a free copy. I am reading a condensed version. I've never read anything quite like it. If it were illustrated by an erotic Japanese artist it would be worth a thousand dollars a copy. I read a few pages at a time before going to sleep; then I fall into one dream after the other, and when I awaken I am like a wet rag. Recommend it to your Japanese friends. The language is fairly simple too. Nothing like the Alexandria Quartet! Oë would probably dig it. And Puko, if it were in Japanese. Maybe it is already, who knows?

That's it for today. Do let me know if you are all right, please.

Your Cocorico
Henry-San

P.S. Do you happen to have in your collection any of Benny Goodman's old records? There's one great one which I heard on tape and I am now trying to get the record. I am also looking for "Fado" records—that's Portuguese songs, very melancholy and dramatic. Not at all like Flamenco music.

MARRIAGE

/\.\/\.\/\.\/\.\/\.\/\.\

Dear Hoki-San—

Got your special delivery letter this morning and was happy to hear from you at last. I realize how busy you must be and feel apologetic some times for all the things I ask you to do for me. Your English is quite good now. The mistakes you make are charming—like earth*quige* for earth*quake*, or "Train has to *speed down*" instead of "slow down." (You can only *speed up*). No matter. I dig you!

Don't let Puko stay too long in Tokyo. Tony will be home the 21st of June, and may only have 2 weeks instead of a month. I want him to have lots of good "bobo"* before he returns to camp.

In my cablegram today I urged you to watch news reports from France. Situation very bad there now. It's like on the eve of a revolution. Foreigners will not be welcome—especially Americans. I know you are eager to travel, to see the world, but from June on the climate is bad in the Middle and Far East. In Hong Kong there will be a shortage of water and possibility of cholera epidemic. The heat will be bad—very humid. Besides, flying from one city to another, and staying just a day or two in each place is no way to see the world. You are only 35 now (or soon)—you have lots of time ahead of you. You will still be young and beautiful at 45 or 55, or maybe 65!!! (I just had a nice letter from Prof. Okamura, saying he saw you on TV and was impressed by your "inexplicable and mysterious beauty." So there!!)

In your letter you say people don't trust Mr. Jin. And your father is worried about him. What has he done, I wonder? Don't *you* trust him either? It always hurts me to hear of people losing confidence in some one. Either you trust someone completely or you don't. If a man is crooked and is going to cheat you, you will not

121

be able to prevent it. I am more disappointed by the poor results of the exhibitions than I would be if Mr. Jin robbed me of my money.

I got one set of *lithos* from Mr. Kubo, by mail. The other set has not come yet. I don't think the lithos are very good—poor color reproduction—cheap work. (Have only seen "the Clown"; not the "Masked Head" which you wrote me about.)

About your operation—strange, isn't it, that one can't sing for 2 or 3 weeks after operation! Did you know that in Belgium they pierce the eyes (blind the bird!) of song birds in order to make it sing better? Maybe you could have the operation here in L.A. (?)

I just got the book Ihara Saikaku—"Koshoku gonin onna."** I will start reading it tonight.

I hope by this time you received my lyrics for the song and the Bonnie and Clyde article, as well as a lot of other things. Today I got a cablegram from Brazil saying there is a possibility of doing the opera of "The Smile." I do hope Tomoko can find an opera conductor in Japan who would like to do it.

I can't understand how our income tax papers got lost on way to Silverman, since I sent them by *certified mail.* Shows you how really bad our postal system is. But if you sign the copies he is sending you it will be OK.

So much for "business details." Oof! I told Val what you wrote about her and she was full of smiles. I get along with her now much better. She is growing up. She listens to me now, not as if I am her father, but like the writer and thinker that I am. She will go back to Aspen before you arrive—it's better that way—but she was very pleased to know you would like her to stay. It's good to have her visit me once in a while, but it's healthier if she doesn't live here permanently. I want to live with you, and you alone. We haven't even begun to live together yet, have we? All I think about is how it will be when you return? Will you be running about like an antelope night after night or—?

MARRIAGE

Somehow, since you left women are calling me up and trying to date me. They seem to smell that you are away and don't give a damn what I do. They all ask me if I am really happy with you? I say Yes, but they don't believe me. There are always rumors floating about that you married me only for your own convenience. Some say that they suspect you have secret lovers—*here and in Japan!!!* My answer is that whether you love me or not, *I love you*. (But I never tell them that my wife doesn't want to hear about love.)

And this reminds me of your letter, your saying you enjoy my letters because they are funny. I must really be a clown! When I say funny things maybe my heart is breaking. I am always waiting to hear you say sincerely, with all your heart—"Henry-San, I love you. I really do!" And until I hear that from your own sweet lips I will be in misery, and nothing I have accomplished in life will have any real meaning for me. To win the Nobel Prize means nothing to me. To have you love me, show it in words and deeds, is all I care about. That is why I often say I don't care if I die tomorrow. But I *would* care if I were sure of your feelings. Does my Hoki-San understand?

My dear wife, I could go on writing you all night. But sometimes I have the dreadful suspicion that you do not read my letters through, that you get bored or in a hurry to go somewhere. What I would give to be looking over your shoulder as you read my letters! To study your face, to know what goes on in your heart! I want so much to see you happy, happy and contented. (Without being spoiled.) You're too big a girl now, too much a woman, to ask to be spoiled all the time. Isn't that so? If God (or whoever) were to say to you tomorrow—"Hoki-San, you can have anything and everything you like!"—would that make you happy? Or would you have sense enough to know that you don't need anything and everything? That you could reply—"Dear God (or whoever), thank you very much, but I am happy just the way I am. Give your riches to someone who needs it!"

Enough! I talk like the Bodhidharma or Lord Krishna, when the fact is I am only Tiny Tim, the Brooklyn boy who fell in love with his soul mate from Shizuoka—by—Tokyo via the Imperial Gardens of Hollywood.

Bless you and love you.

* sex.
** "Five Sensual Women."

Henry-San

/\\.\\./\\./\\./\\./\\.\\

Saturday May 25, 1968

Dear Hoki Bellissima!

The last three photos you sent are just out of this world! Is it possible I have such a beautiful wife? Your eyes especially are so dreamy, so soft and dewy, and your mouth is the perfect mouth, and you look thinner in the face, good, and the hair-do suits you perfectly. Bravo! Come home looking just like that and I will be your devoted slave.

("Anata no hitomini niji O mita")

Noko was here with a friend from Hawaii—Mary Harimoto(?) Noko says they warned her, when she got visa extended, not to work. I told her to come here and stay with us soon as possible. But she just rented the place at S. Elden, moved into another apartment, NO. 1, so. . . . ? If she gets caught working it's bad for me.

About one in the morning Mr. Jin's secretary telephoned from Tokyo to say that Mr. Jin had sent me $3,960.00 direct to my bank. That is what money they have collected so far. Strange to call me up at that hour to tell me that. Mr. Jin is also giving me 1,000 of the catalogs as a gift. I am trying to think up some way to sell them, maybe for two or three dollars each.

124

MARRIAGE

Val left yesterday. Never saw her looking or behaving better. We really got along wonderfully. She is now soft and gentle and smiling and happy—like she was as a little girl. Told me to send you her love, and this time I am sure she meant it. She also asked if you could bring home a two ounce bottle of a French perfume called *Envol*, put out by Lancome—thought it would be cheaper in Japan. If you don't have room for all the gifts you are bringing, forget about it, and I will get it for her here. But I'll tell her you got it in Tokyo.

Val has a whole closet full of good clothes that she doesn't want any more. If you know any one her size who is very poor and would appreciate having them, let me know. I don't want to give them to the Salvation Army.

Got your long letter special delivery and was very pleased to read all the news, especially about your songs. Joe was just here and I was asking him about the Bossa Nova beat and he says it's great, what he likes best in songs. I can understand the trouble you must have had trying to translate my song; when you come back I am sure we will be able to knock out some tunes together. It would be great if you could write the music and not give it to a song writer to do. I have now made good friends with Mr. Kaper who writes much of the music for the films, songs especially. He is coming next week for dinner and to play ping pong. If we needed any help or ideas I feel he could give us them. He's a great old friend of Mr. Gimpel and an amusing man. Did I understand you to say that these records you are making are for sale in America as well as Japan? How do they do that? Do they have records in two languages or what? Your royalties (15%) are very very good—unusual. (I mailed you special delivery my song in my handwriting, as you asked.) Funny about the "garden door". I meant to tell you when I sent the lyrics that you could substitute gate or some other word for that, but forgot. I put it in because I was thinking of how I first saw you (at Siegel's) coming through the gate in their garden. (It was *not* a door.) Do you realize that you look ever so much more beautiful, and younger, now than when I first met you? What is the secret? I think the way you did your hair, in the photo, has a lot to do with giving your head just the right shape. You remember I told you when you had your hair cut (before going to France) that you looked more attractive that way? (Puko also looked wonderful in the photo of the two of you.) The only photos of you I don't really care much about are the ones in that magazine, where you are posing with bikini and brassiere. It would have been better if you had posed stark naked. The brassiere, for one thing, destroys all sexiness. Also, you look too "demure". (Look that up in the dictionary.)

The news about cancellation of exhibitions was not so heartbreaking for me. The truth is that it was my fault! But I think you did wonderfully just the same and I am deeply grateful to you. I will be curious to hear about the real Mr. Jin, how he makes a living. I'm glad to read that you are not mad (with him or anybody) but glad that you know what life is like over there, even if it is horrible. That's the way of the world most everywhere— everywhere where money counts, at least.

So you like *Modigliani*'s paintings? He paints nudes too, you know. But all his women have those long necks—rather stylized. He had a terrible life—I know all about him and his work.

The man who is going to produce my play on stage wrote me that there is a chance the Theatre Guild in N. Y. will do something about it—with their subscribers. Will explain more when I see you, but it sounds promising. Won't be put on till September now, but in a bigger, better way.

By the way, if Mr. Jin has more money to pay me, please let him send it direct, will you? Better for my accounting. Be sure you get the correct numbers (my number and date) of those sold, yes? It's very very nice of your father to want to buy three paintings. But can he afford to do that? Don't let him do it just to help us. If his rich friend wants to buy I won't object.

I must make myself some dinner now. Have a lot of leftovers. Will be seeing Saichyo fight next week.

Now I find the correct way to write this Nam. . . . Like this: "Namu myo horen gekyo!" Say it fifty times a day. It is really bringing me good luck all the time. The best it can bring me will be *you* (with a rainbow in your eyes).

And that's it for today. Take good care of yourself. Come home safe and sound and looking like the mysterious princess of the Land of the Rising Sun which you are. I love you.

Henry Sancho Panza

Thank you for always calling me darling—I mean "saint"!

On June 14, 1968, Hoki returned home to Henry in the Pacific Palisades. He did not write to her again until she returned to Japan in September of that year.—Ed.

/\.V.\/\/\.V.\/\\

Sept. 8th, 1968

Dear Hoki-San—

In two days it will be one year since our first marriage. Congratulations! Weren't you lucky to find a man like Henry Miller? Now to see if we can last the second year, eh? In the first round, to use the language of boxing, one simply feels the other person out. No hard punches, no K.O. Just sparring. Maybe the second round will be more exciting. What do you think?

We went to see Saicho (fighter) train the other day. Had my photo taken with him in the gym—for a Japanese sports magazine. Maybe you'll see it.

The other night a friend of yours (an American) called Puko four times in succession at four in the morning. He was dead drunk and refused to give his name. Then he threatened to come to the house—which frightened her. I got out my sharp machete in case he broke the door down. But he didn't come. Next day he called and apologized.

Nothing much new here except that we seem to have a good time every day.

I got your letter from Tokyo and am glad to hear all is going well. Keep me posted on your doings.

And please ask Tomoko where she sent my text (from Holiday Mag.)—has it been accepted or not?

I must stop here. Some one just came to take me to dinner. More in next.

Love
Henry-San

Cuando Merda Tivev Pobre Nasco Seur Cu

/\\.\\/.\\/.\\/.\\/.\\/\\

October '68

Dear Hoki-San, Sama, Samadhi and precious Omanko:

So glad to get your two letters together this morning. Have waited a long, long time. This evening—soon now—I'll try phoning you again. It should be between ten and twelve in the morning in Tokyo. I didn't realize you were depressed and having such a hard time of it or I would have written sooner and oftener. To tell the truth I was peeved at you for not writing me even if I hadn't written you. But as I said in my last letter, it's foolish to play this game, don't you think so? When you come home we must get closer together. I need you as much as you need me—*or don't you need me?* Sometimes, many times, that's the impression you give me. Puko has tried to explain your behavior to me and I think I understand better now what has been the trouble between us. I miss you very much, even though I didn't see much of you in this first year of married life. But please don't think that acting this way is the way to keep me interested. It is just the opposite. Stay close to me,

128

show me some real affection and you will mean more to me than you ever imagined. Enough of this for the moment. . . .

I am writing you again tomorrow, as I must get this off in a hurry. You will find a check from the California State for a refund on our income tax. Would you please sign your name, as given on the check, under mine, and mail it back *air, registered mail.*

Puko has been taking good care of me, and now gives me that long promised massage, which is really wonderful and makes me feel like a new man. As you know, she is leaving for Europe on the 15th and will be gone three weeks. I will miss her. She has a wonderful character, a beautiful soul, and I think it is a great compliment to you to possess such a wonderful person as a friend.

Mr. Yokoo was here the other day and said he saw you almost every day, that you were enjoying yourself, and that your songs over the radio were making a hit. He is a strange person, isn't he? A mixture of little boy and wise old man, with a sadness underneath. He dresses like a dandy too. I told him some things about himself and his childhood, which came to me intuitively, and I also made predictions about his future.

Puko met John Drury again and went to the studios with him and Mako. He's a very nice young man, but a little too simple, too naive and boyish, I think, for Puko. (I hope she doesn't fall in love or marry George G., unless she marries him just to stay in America.) We also went to see her lawyer and decided afterwards to do nothing—all too complicated and risky. As it is, she has a multiple visa and can travel back and forth from Japan as often as she likes until 1971. So, why worry? By that time she may have met some one she would really like to marry. O.K.? I must add that she began painting in oil recently and the three portraits she finished are, in my opinion, simply wonderful. I hope she will keep on painting. She has great talent, and I mean it sincerely.

Oh yes, some one sent me an article-interview about you in a woman's magazine. I am still waiting to get all the details translated. There were photos of you at the piano, one in pajamas, singing, and the other in a bathing suit or it looked like one. Very coy.

In this article you are quoted as saying you don't care about men except as "escorts and sponsors". Ha ha! And then there is some stuff about why you married me, which I guess was invented by the editor.

Tom Smothers of Smothers Bros. was here Saturday and we had a good time—ping pong and all. Puko seemed to like him very much. He is a very serious young man, and not really so funny, at least in private. I am going to do a short bit with him on his show —but will do it in the studio and not on stage.

Last night we went to dinner with Johnny Robinson (!), his girl friend Ray ———, whom you knew in Tokyo—once a strip tease artist, I understand. Not a bad girl, or woman. Asked about you warmly. Johnny looks older than before—like an extinct volcano. But very much the gentleman. I flattered the pants off him, about his generosity and kindness. I think now that he is a very well meaning individual—not what I first took him to be.

If you have a chance, Hoki, try to pick up some more copies of those two books of mine you brought back from Japan, remember? I wrote the publishers for copies but they never answered. The only Japanese who answers promptly is Kubo, bless his soul.

When Puko comes home today (she is with Jerry Ray now) I will see if she can find the Holiday article. If she can't I'll send another one. When you send it out let me know to which magazine, will you please?

And now I must stop. In a few hours I hope to hear your voice on the telephone. I do hope you are well and happier now—and that you didn't catch pneumonia floating in the river. (A real river or just fake river?)

And now all my love and lots more. Write me when you can and I'll keep writing you. If you know where I can write you after the 13th let me know, eh? You're always in my heart.

Henry-San

P.S. Next time you take photo at shower please drop the towel!!!

MARRIAGE

/\/\.\/\./\./\/\.\

Oct. 15th 1968
(1oc A.M.)

Dear Hoki-San—

I am giving this to Puko to mail at the airport this morning as
she leaves for Europe. I'm going to miss her. And I feel sorry that
she has to visit Europe with such an insufferable bore as G———
I can't stand that man. He would drive me crazy in a few hours.
We went to dinner with him one night and it was painful—I
couldn't get back home quickly enough.

I hope you get these few words when you pass through Tokyo
on the 20th. I haven't received any more letters from you since we
telephoned and I am very anxious to know how you are. I think
Tomoko must be some kind of reckless idiot to let you work when
you were in such a bad condition. (Especially to let you "float in
the river.") She sounds just as bad, or worse to me, than a Hollywood agent. Hasn't she any feelings at all?

Today Nobuko came and asked if she could come and stay here
until she leaves for Japan—her roommate left so she had to give up
the apartment. Naturally I said yes. Now I am wondering if you
are bringing your youngest sister back with you?

We only use your Jaguar now to go to the neighborhood stores.
There are too many leaks (in the fluids) to risk longer trips. Also,
Puko says you are not insured for any driver but yourself. So it is
better to keep it in the garage until you return and sell it.

Tonight Puko told me you are not earning much money in spite
of all the work you are doing. I am sorry for you, because of such
a waste of time, money, energy, etc. etc.

Yesterday we received a package you sent with trays and dishes
—and in the package are several packs of *innocent* photos—"My
Darling." Did you mean them for me or for Tony? (or maybe Joe

Gray, huh?) I am really waiting for a photo of *you* in your birthday suit, if you know what that means. Don't disappoint me.

Just read another interview with you in some Japanese (woman's) magazine. Same old story, eh? But there was one thing you said which did interest me, and that was that Oriental and Caucasian couples deceive themselves when they look for "mystery" in one another. The only mystery is that which we create ourselves. And yet—if you stop to think seriously, *all is mystery*, including even a blade of grass. We don't know how or why anything is, though we think we are very clever with our long-winded explanations, scientific, metaphysical, cosmological, religious or whatever. Do you agree? So, even if you are not as mysterious as I pretended you were, you are still a mystery. (and so is Henry-San, don't forget!) The strangest thing about all this is that even when we are no longer a mystery to others we remain a mystery to ourselves. Oof! Let's get on to something else . . .

The important thing is—do you miss me as much as I miss you? Whom did you have lunch with yesterday? How many new suits of clothes have you bought? Is the toilet paper always soft and silky? Are you getting fatter or slimmer? (Puko has just discovered that "slim" means thin in an interesting way.) Her English, by the way, has improved quite a bit since you are away.

It seems that you and Puko will be returning about the same time, maybe the same day. And if Nobuko and your other sister are also here then, it will be quite a harem! I will have to find some young studs to keep you all happy and fertilized, what!

And now to sleep and to dream. I will try to meet you in my dreams, though I don't know where you are. But if the astronauts can find Mars, Venus, Jupiter and the moon, I ought to be able to find *you*. And findings is keepings, as they say. So, good-night, think of me and come home safe and sound.

Your
Henry-San

MARRIAGE

/\/\/\/\/\/\

Dear Hoki-San, = Song bird, Love bird!

I can't tell you how disappointed I am not to have had a word from you in all this time—not since we talked over the phone. What can be the trouble? If you were ill I would think that you would let me know. If you are traveling surely you must be able to find time to write a post card now and then, if not a letter.

All I can imagine, from this end, is that you did not receive the letters I mailed you before leaving Tokyo. Today you should be passing through Tokyo again, I believe, and I do hope you found my letters, especially the one with the check from the Income Tax (a refund for over $1,400.00) which I asked you to sign and mail back to me by *registered* mail.

The other night on TV I saw a short documentary on Kysushu and all the volcanos there and hot springs. You were there while I was watching the film, and I was wondering where you might be and if you found time to get to the countryside. Last night we saw the film you made in Tokyo when you were last there. There were lots of interesting shots and I especially enjoyed seeing your big family. I think I recognized your youngest sister, whom I mistook at first for Nobuko. She looks very pretty. What a lot of children there were. And who owned that big American car? What surprised me more than anything was the color of the houses; I had always thought they were very drab, plain, brownish looking. But many of the houses looked quite gay. And the temple shots were very good. I caught just one little glimpse of you—only once. The film ran very fast and it was a little dizzying to watch; maybe we didn't turn it at the right speed. But the scenes were well taken, I thought.

Naturally I am dying to know what is happening. How does it go with the group you are with? Are you happy or disgusted? At an exhibition of Varda's collages the other day I met a friend of Anaïs Nin (a Japanese scientist married to a Japanese woman

133

writer) and he said he saw you on television in Tokyo not long ago, singing, and that you were very good. Then some one wrote me from Japan about a television show, a serial, suspense drama, in which a man is about to be killed by gangsters, and he says: "Don't kill me yet. I have lots of work to do. I must write about Henry Miller." Funny, what?

I haven't heard from Puko-san yet but no doubt you have. I hope she is enjoying herself, though how she can with that piece of dead wood, George G., I don't understand. No doubt she will meet some interesting young man on the side and sneak off with him for a good time. We now have two more prospects for her to meet when she returns. One of them is a retired millionaire, about 40 years old, I understand. Which reminds me—did you read about Jacqueline Kennedy marrying that Greek ship owner? To me it read like feeding a siren to a vulture. I think, and I believe the world feels the same way, that it is a pity she did not make a more romantic alliance—this marriage sounds like a business arrangement: two dynasties joining up to perpetuate their billions of dollars and all that.

I'm going to hold this letter till tomorrow morning's mail arrives, in the hope I will find a letter from you in the box, and then add some more words to this. If I don't hear from you very soon I'll take it you don't give a damn, and if that's the case, well. . . . . . ? ? ? ? ? ? Meanwhile I look at your photos and talk to you long distance over the ether waves. Please don't stuff your ears!

5.00 P.M. Monday

P.S. Waited all day for a special delivery letter or telegram or something. But nothing has come. I'll have to repeat "Nam myoho _____." more often—maybe 50 times a day, or 100 or 500!!! Somehow I just can't believe that I can be so *un*important to you as to not even merit a post card. In Paris you mailed postcards and letters by the ton. Now silence, nothing but silence. The silence makes my ears ring!! If I don't hear from you very soon I'll retire to a monastery and live the rest of my life out in total silence.

Enough now

MARRIAGE

Do you sleep well?
Do you eat well?
Do you dream well?
Do you sing well?
What don't you do well? I'm curious to know.
P.P.S. Puko's latest "amant" just received a postcard from her from
Paris. Quick service! Nobuko never came to stay after all.

/\.\/\.\/\.\/\.\/\.\/\

Midnight Oct. 24th 1968

Star of the Orient, Hoki no koibito!*

Kwannon-Sama** was good to me today! All day today and
yesterday and the day before I have been saying "Nam myoho
renge kyo!"—hundreds of times. All to make Hoki-San get in
touch with me. And tonight your lovely voice calls me from Kyoto
—blessed be the name! It was like hearing from Venus or Mars.
You always sound so far away on the telephone, even if you're only
calling from An heim chez le Duc de Guise (or whatever his real
name is.)

It's such a long time since I heard from you last. Such a very very
long time since I saw you and embraced you. Just today I discovered in my desk a beautiful snapshot of you taken in front of our
house—by Puko. I laid it on my desk to look at and to talk to you,
no matter how far away you might be. And, like magic, you answered me this evening. I was so surprised and happy I didn't
know what to say. (I never am good at talking to you on the telephone am I?) Afterwards, after I have hung up, I talk to you like
a madman. Then I tell you all the things I meant to say—but too
late.

Even now with pen in hand, I feel shy and awkward. I don't
think I have ever really talked to you the way I really feel. It seems

that just when I am ready to pour out my heart you get nervous or restless or shy or whatever and you are like a bird trying to fly out of my hand. I feel lost, I lose my tongue. I don't understand why you want to run away. My dear, dear Hoki, I want so much to get close to you, not just to hold you in my arms, but to hold you in my heart, to make our two hearts beat as one. Perhaps this sounds sentimental to you. I can't help it if it does. I am not ashamed of my feelings. In our best moments, when we get serious and honest with one another, I feel that we really belong to one another, that we have a life to live together, that we can make one another happier and richer in spirit. If this is not true then we ought to separate. I don't want to live a lie, and I don't think you want to either. I don't want to play games with you—it's too childish, too silly. Please when you come home be my wife, my friend, my dream come true. I need you, Hoki darling, I need you to make my life what I always wanted it to be. I want to believe in you as I hope you believe in me. We must believe and trust one another, else everything is a farce. If only I could write you in Japanese! Maybe then I could reach your heart. Maybe then I could say poetically what I now say so crudely. When I look at your photos, and I have so many of you, I think sometimes I am looking at a flower—so delicate, so sensitive I feel your soul to be, oh yes, I know another Hoki, who is hard, practical, demanding, sarcastic, moody, whimsical, unpredictable. But it is not the real Hoki-San. That is the Hoki who had to learn to meet the world, to make her way, to save herself from destruction. (Does my Hoki follow me?)

Nobody ever hurt Henry-San more than Hoki-San. But Henry-San loves Hoki-San and he tries to understand, to forgive, to accept her for what she is. It is easy to love an angel, but it takes a greater love to stick with one's Hoki-San. And in the end Hoki-San will bring Henry-San more happiness, more joy, more fulfillment than any of God's angels. That is how much Henry-San believes in Hoki-San. (Do I make sense, my Bakari?)***

Tonight you are in Kyoto, you say. I try my best to picture you there. Always I am struggling to see you as you are, where you are.

"The night has a thousand eyes, the day but one." (Lord Byron).
I am searching always for that one, that beautiful, blazing sun
without which my life has no meaning.

You said you would send me a gift from Kyoto. Did you mean—
Kwannon? The only gift I want from you is *you*. Give me your
heart. Put it in my hands. I will nourish it and cherish it.

And now, dear Hoki, enough. Good night, sweet dreams—and
dream true!

I will call you on the 30th, which is the 31st in Japan, and if I
don't get you I will call you on the 31st American calendar. And if
you find time before that to write me or cable me I will know what
I never dare ask you to say—that you love me. Be all the things you
are, come home soon and safely, and let us pray that nothing will
make us part.

(Do you see now what a little telephone call will do?)

Your Henry-San

* "my lover."
** a Goddess of Mercy.
*** "my only one."

/\/.\/\/\/.\/.\/\

Sunday Oct. 27th

Dear Hoki-San—

No letter from you yet, but I feel it coming. I'm coming too, just
thinking about it. (In Japanese they say "going" not "coming".)
The other day when Dr. Natanabe gave me an injection for my hip
he said it contained an aphrodisiac. I thought he was joking at first
but now I begin to realize it's true. I feel like doing "onani"* all
the time. But then I remember what the doctor told you—though I

137

don't believe it. Incidentally, what news about O-Manko-Sama**
now? Anything new? And where is the photo I asked you to send
me—the one without the towel? I am waiting for it. Those other
"koi-bito"*** photos you sent me were for teen–agers. Reminds me
of Playboy Magazine, not the Swedish magazine, remember?

This afternoon I am taking Mako and Michiyo to Siegels for ping
pong. I have to meet the head of Paramount there about my
"Cancer" film. It's soon time for them to start production. In a day
or two Bob Snyder will show me the film (part of it) which we did
in the little cafe on the Rue Monffetard—you and I playing ping
pong. It took all these months for Pathé (Paris) to send the film.
When you return I want you to pose for me—nude or semi-nude,
according to your mood—so that I can have some water colors to
look at when you are gone. (No more long trips, or I'll get myself
a concubine!)

I enclosed a clipping about the student riots in Japan. Was your
brother hurt or arrested? Have you seen him again? I think I
caught a glimpse of him in the family group you took with your
8mm camera—yes? Rather good-looking?

You are the good-looking one, from the 12th century, when the
moon was full and life was gay. Before the Tokudana period (?)
It's still very warm here—almost 90 in the sun. I am going for a
swim now. I'll think about you as I swim around. No onani business!
Just love. How's that?

Write soon and oftener. Make the last few days of your absence
happy ones for me. Try! (I won't accept any more excuses.)

Until then, be your very best. "Turn on, tune in, drop out!" Play
it cool but keep the fires burning.

Your
Henry-San
of
the 2nd year
of holy wedlock!!!

* sex.
** vagina.
*** sweetheart.

MARRIAGE

/\\/\\/\\/\\/\\/\\/\\

Thursday 10/31/68

Dear Hoki-San—

A quick one before dashing to the doctor for my weekly check up. Though it was good to talk to you on the phone, I was alarmed by the sound of your coughing and choking. Do let me know how you feel in your next letter. Today will be the first day in weeks that I don't swim in the pool. Hearing you cough so much on the phone last night I woke up coughing too. (In Australia when the woman goes to bed with labor pains—to have a baby—the husband also goes to bed and has pains. *Sympathy pains.* That's me!)

Try to rest up before you start homeward. Maybe it will still be warm enough here for you to use the pool. We keep it 86 to 88.

Hope you kept some kind of record of your expenses (and all the bills) for Silverman. Also hope the check you are mailing me doesn't get lost in the mails.

I'm waiting for you to return to get fresh inspiration. Without you I can't do any real writing or painting. So, be good to me, stay near me, love me in your own sweet way—which means "as best as you can." Services rendered gratuitously will be appreciated by miserable honorable husband. My best to Kwannon and to the omanko Extraordinaire.

No time for any jokes today. Treat yourself like a queen and, even if you have to turn yourself inside out, write me some real, honest to God words from the heart.

Henry-San

P.S. I forgot to say—*I still love you.*

/\\.\\/\\.\\/\\.\\/\\.\\/\\.\\/\\.\\

Saturday 3.30 P.M.
11/2/68

Still no letter, no check, no nothing from Hoki-San. I'm making this short as I don't want the pigeon-carrier to be overburdened and arrive too late.

I hope you will not forget to bring me some token of the Goddess Kwannon—maybe a replica of her as Irobotoka or Hitohada or the Immei Kwannon—all of which you must be familiar with. I like the idea that Kwannon is sometimes thought of as "a merciful cunt."

I enclose a clipping about one of the TV films you made—in which you were "the guest star" (!)

Maybe by nightfall a letter will come.

Onegai shimasu.   O Yasumi nasai!   Itadaki masu.*

(Dans mon ame je nage toujours.)**

Henry-San
or
Samson Agonistes

* "Do me this favor. Goodnight. I'm hoping to receive one." (a letter)
** In my soul I am still swimming.

Part III
DISSILLUSION

EDITOR'S NOTE: *In 1969 Henry wrote Hoki thirty-four letters. She returned home from another visit to Japan in December of that year, and they finally separated in May of 1970. From 1970 to 1975, there is a desultory correspondence—birthday notes and so forth.*
In January Hoki has gone to Hawaii for a vacation.

$$\wedge\!\!\wedge\!\!\wedge\!\!\wedge\!\!\wedge\!\!\wedge\!\!\wedge$$

Jan. 4th 1969

Dear Hoki-San

I've finally come to the conclusion that there is no sense in our living together any longer as man and wife. We have never been man and wife in the real sense. You have never shown me any love or affection. You run away from me when I approach you—as if I were some monster. You seem only to care about yourself, your security. We live like two strangers. I had hoped during these short two years of marriage that you would change one day, but apparently you can't or won't.

I am not going to blame you. You can't help being what you are. But I can't continue to live such a meaningless life. For me love is the most important thing in life. For you it is unimportant apparently.

DISILLUSION

I think therefore that we should separate. When you return I'll
arrange about a divorce. Maybe we'll both be happier that way.

Henry

/\\/\\/\\/\\/\\/\\

Hoki-San—

Tonight I feel absolutely miserable. I tried to phone you but there
was no answer. Today I got your postcard. I can still hear your voice
over the phone telling me you had mailed me a card—as if you had
presented me with a 24-carat diamond!

How unhappy you have made me, ever since—and even before—
our marriage. Never once have you shown me any love, any affection, any consideration—not even the respect due me as your husband. You have gone your own sweet way, doing only what pleased
you, expecting devotion but showing none yourself. A spoiled, dis-
contented child, thoroughly selfish, and acting as if she were a
prisoner in her own home.

Being alone, always alone, I think and think about our life
together—or rather our life apart. And I ask myself—why did she
ever consent to marry me? Was it only to get a permanent visa to
remain in America? Almost everything you have asked for—with
the exception of a mink coat—I have given you. But you show no
appreciation—only boredom, discontent. You can't bear to remain
at home of an evening. If you do it is only to cut your toe nails,
shampoo your hair or some such nonsense.

You go out when you please, where you please, and with whom
you please. And you take it for granted that I am quite content to
stay home and watch TV. You leave, saying "I'll see you later", but
you haven't the slightest intention of coming home in time to "see
me later." You stay out all night and get drunk and you don't

even let me know where you are, or whom you are with. You act as if I should understand and treat it lightly. You never think that perhaps I get up every hour or two of the night to go and see if the car is in the garage. You simply don't give a damn. And you think I like that sort of behavior. You think it makes me miss you, want you all the more. What a sad mistake you make! With every callous, willful, selfish move you make you drive me further away from you. You make me distrust you, disgust me. What I once called love has turned into something much much less—infatuation. And even that you are killing by your silly, stupid behavior.

So where are we? What sense does this marriage make? I thought when I married you that I would protect you, give you the kind of life you wished. You said always that you hated your work at the piano bar. But you go off to Japan, work your ass off for nothing, leave me $3,000 in the hole, and pretend that it was very important. You have no ambition, you don't like to work, and yet you behave as if you were a star. Have you ever looked at yourself honestly? Have you ever dropped your false pride and seen yourself as the human being you are? Have you ever thought for one minute about anybody but yourself?

I think of the night before you left for Hawaii. You were out all night, drunk, I understand. I had been up every hour of the night, looking for you, wondering where you were. I meet you at breakfast time just as you are coming home from the bus station. You tell me you just took your father to the bus. You don't say anything about being out all night. You think perhaps I don't know. No need to make excuses—Henry-San was sound asleep. But Henry-San has never been sound asleep when you are out of a night. He has never had one night's good sound sleep when you have been out—and how many, many nights you have left him alone!!! (Including our two marriage nights) And this is really unforgivable.

And this Hawaiian trip. So important to show Sumiko Hawaii! But Sumiko is only there two or three days. So it is not Sumiko you worried about—but your own whimsical desire to have a vacation. It is true when I called you Monday to find out when you were returning, I said—"Stay as long as you like. Stay a month, if you wish." And why did I say that? Because I felt that it was better for you to stay where you were happy than to come back home and feel miserable with me.

And then, as if I were a child who could be made happy with a candy bar, you tell me gleefully that you sent me a post card. How generous of you. What a regal treat! You went to the great trouble of going to a shop, buying a card, writing a few trivial words, buying a postage stamp, walking to the post office and dropping it in the slot. How very wonderful! How tender! I ought to get down on my knees and thank you, oughtn't I? Domo Arigato,* Hoki-Sama! What noblesse!

Do you begin to see what you really look like? Do you think I exaggerate? Woman, you haven't heard a thousandth part of what I could tell you. There isn't anything you've said or done that I forget. There isn't any promise that you broke that I have forgotten. I know you right down to the ground. Even your tears tell me of your insincerity. You have never fooled me. I have been patient with you, that's all. I hoped against hope. But it has all been in vain. You'll never change. You have no heart. You don't even have the integrity of a whore. You're a cheat through and through— and everyone knows it, including yourself.

Henry-San

P.S. Of all my experiences with women, good and bad ones, this with you is the very worst.

* Many thanks.

DISILLUSION

/\/\\/\\/\\/\\/\

Dear Hoki-San

Welcome back home! How are you? I had to go to Mr. Gimpel's Master Class this evening but will see you in the morning.

Riko was here the other day and though I didn't ask her any questions she started telling me things about you—very nice things and one surprising thing—that you really and truly loved me.

If that is true then it is harder than ever to understand why you refuse to show it. Why you always run away from me when I want to put my arms around you. Don't tell me Japanese women don't show love that way, because I know better.

I would never have written to you as I did if I did not feel desperate. It's not divorce I am interested in so much as having your love—and affection. But, as I wrote you, if you can't show me this then it seems the only thing to do is to separate. Believe me, that would hurt me as much or more than it hurts you. Much as I resent the way you treat me I can't help loving you. And it's a terrible thing to kill one's love. No decent man or woman wants to do that. But, my dear Hoki, you must know as well as I that two people who profess to love each other can certainly find a way to express their love and share it. I believe what you told Riko. All that I ask of you is that you demonstrate it.

You have puzzled me and frustrated me and hurt me more than any woman I have ever known, yet somehow I feel that you never wilfully intended to do so. Maybe I am clumsy, awkward, say and do the wrong things, but my heart is in the right place, my heart yearns for you. I would like you to be my wife forever. It is up to you now, I have spoken.

Have a good sleep, and may the good Lord bless and protect you.

Henry-San

/٠\/٠\/٠\/٠\/٠\/٠\/٠\

Friday 3.30 A.M.

Hoki-San—

Once again I'm furious with you. You have the gall to tell me tonight that you sacrificed *four nights* since you came back from Hawaii—four nights of boredom, just to please me. And on top of it you say you could have stayed home and enjoyed yourself, you who never want to stay home because it bores you.

Your spoiled, selfish attitude not only makes me angry, it disgusts me. I feel that I am living with a heartless little monster. Never will I ask you again to go out with me to meet my friends or do me a favor, nor do I want to see or entertain any of your friends. Let's go our separate ways until things get so bad that we can't stand the sight of each other and we separate for good.

The letters I was going to give you I am destroying. And as for going to Paris with you, or anywhere else, out of the question. Why should I make myself miserable? What can you do for me that I can't do myself? What have you ever done to show me that you are my wife?

I repeat—I am absolutely disgusted with you. I don't care what happens any more. I've lost all interest in living with you. I could pick up any whore in the street and receive better treatment than I get from you. I wonder sometimes if you know what you say and do or if you are walking in your sleep.

Henry-San

Later in January, Hoki's father and step-mother came again to stay with the Millers.

DISILLUSION

/\/\/\/\/\/\

January 1969

Hoki-San—

I'm very angry with you. You should not have run out on me as
you did. I can't forgive you. You say I kiss everybody. All I want
is to kiss *you*. But you never show me any love, any affection. You're
not even jealous. What am I to do?

I'm tired of all this foolishness. It's like child's play. Either you
act like a woman or—I love you and I make excuses for you, for
the way you treat me—but you go too far. You think only about
yourself, what *you* want and so forth.

If you really love me, show it, prove it to me. Otherwise I must
find somebody else. I can't go on living this way with you. It's
crazy.

You were wonderful tonight. But I didn't feel that you did it for
me. You wanted to get drunk. You got drunk. But where did it get
you?

I am not going to baby sit for your father and step-mother. I am
not going to sit home and wait for you to come home at any hour
of the night or morning. I am *not* a Japanese wife.

If you don't like the way we are living then let us get a divorce.
I'm sick of living in this crazy way.

Henry-San

*In June, Hoki goes to New York, where she will sail to England
and thence to Paris. Henry plans to join her either in London or
France.*

/\.\/\.\/\.\/\.\/\.\/\.\/\.\

Monday 6/2/69

Dear Hoki-San—

Enclosing special delivery letter from Japan. If you call me Wednesday I'll tell you what Oko wrote—Riko comes tomorrow morning to read it. Was great to hear your voice—you sounded excited, happy, very much alive. Bravo!

I'll write you to London—c/o my publishers, Calder and Boyars —you have address and telephone number. I am rushing out in a minute to eat at Gimpels. I have invitations for dinner every day, but I don't want to be bored, so I sometimes cook for myself.

I was surprised—and yet not!—not to get even a post card from you. But now I look forward to getting a real letter, eh what what?

I have so much to tell you I don't know where to begin. But you can imagine a lot, yes?

You mentioned "Calcutta." But did you see "I am Curious (Yellow)"? "Tropic of Cancer" will probably be tame by comparison—just natural, healthy fucking, which is now old hat.

I hope you enjoy the boat trip. I'm sure you'll be one of the "star" passengers. When you sing for the crew please sing "Fly me to the Moon" and I'll get it by radar. Stay well, think of me now and then, *and write me!!!*

Much love.

Your Henry-San

And hello to darling Puko-San, my *un*faithful concubine No. 1.

DISILLUSION

∧∧∧∧∧∧
`.∨.∨.∨.∨.∨.∨.`

(To Hoki in London)

June 6th 1969

Dear Hoki-San—

Not much to tell you, except that I'm busier than ever now. Paris-Match (magazine) comes tomorrow for interview and photos. Then Life mag. Then I read and correct long script for Bradley's book. Ping pong at Kaper's Sunday afternoon. Another film showing for Tommy Smothers, who *may* let us rent the theatre where "Hair" is showing on the off night—once a week. (To show our documentary.)

At this writing, it looks as if I'll leave here the 24th or 25th of June, go to Montreal, then to London, and be in Paris July 1st. We haven't yet found a suitable apt. in Paris. If we don't get one in time I'll go to the Hotel le Royal on the Blvd. Raspail—my old hotel. They have the rooms we want and at a good price.

I'm writing Mr. Calder in day or two to fix definite date for my coming to London. I would go on TV and meet the press too.

Lisa Lu came last night with beautiful Chinese meal for seven people. Shushuen is in Monte Carlo presently, but no one has her address. Her film went to Cannes but not for a prize.

Next letter will be more personal—this sounds like a business letter, forgive me. I can picture you on the boat at the piano singing your repertoire in X-major.

Keep me posted. Lots of love. Enjoy yourself.

Henry-San

P.S. Enclose letter and post card from Oko.

/\\.\\/\\\\/\\\\/\\\\.\\

(copy for Hoki)

THE PLEASURES OF RE-READING   (*for Yomiuri Shimbun*)

One of the few advantages of old age is the pleasure, a very keen, rewarding pleasure, of being able to read one's favorite books after a lapse of thirty, fifty, even seventy years. Only a few months ago I decided to read *Cuore* (*The Heart of a Boy*) by the Italian, Edmondo de Amicis. Every page brought back reminiscences of the first reading, when I was nine or ten years of age. I had the same emotions as I did almost seventy years ago, plus the critical acumen of the veteran writer which I am.

It seems to me now that the literary fare offered youngsters a half century ago or more was of a higher standard than that which they are nourished on today. I think of writers like Rider Haggard and Henryk Sienkiewicz, the Polish author, and of George Alfred Henty, the English author who wrote historical novels for young people. Every Christmas I would find under the Christmas tree eight or ten of his books which I devoured like a ravenous wolf. I must have read over seventy-five of his novels by the time I was twelve years old. The very names of these books gave me a thrill: *The Cat of Bubastes*, for instance, or *The Lion of the North* (in which I met Wallenstein, who was an astrologer as well as a warrior and diplomat.) Certainly I learned more about history from Henty's works than I did from all the school books I was obliged to read. It was not until many years later, when I discovered Oswald Spengler —his *Decline of the West*—that my interest in history was revived.

I don't know how it is in Japan, but in America I have the impression that we seldom re-read books. Here books (paper backs) are relatively cheap, easily discarded, and quickly forgotten. We do not take pride in exhibiting our personal library, as do the French and Germans, for example. We do not bring our paper backs to a binder and have them bound according to our taste. Nor do I encounter people who are seeking for books they read years ago in order to savour them anew. As with buildings, cars, clothes, wives and mistresses, here nothing lasts very long. We are the very opposite of the ancient Egyptians, who thought in terms of eternity. With us nothing is precious, nothing inspires awe or reverence.

Speaking of awe and reverence, of love and worship, of beauty and imagination, there comes to mind the name of a once most popular British woman writer whose pen name was Marie Corelli. For twelve years or more she outsold any other British writer, man or woman; this was the period around the turn of the century. As a teen-ager I had read secretly (in bed) her *Vendetta* and *Thelma* and *Wormwood*. By the time I was twenty-one I had read most of her work. It was only about twenty-five years later, in Paris, when her name popped up in a conversation about reincarnation, that my interest in her was rekindled. At the time of her great success she was a contemporary of such writers as G.K. Chesterton, Rider Haggard and Oscar Wilde; Wilde, as a matter of fact, paid open tribute to her, despite the fact that she was regarded by the critics of her day as a very mediocre writer.

I began my second reading of her with such titles as *The Master Christian, The Sorrows of Satan, The Soul of Lilith and Life Everlasting*. With all that was said against her, and there is undoubtedly much to criticize in her writing, I nevertheless found her wonderful, inspiring, possessed of a great imagination and an exaltation which few writers in any epoch seem to possess. I admired particularly the manner in which she wrote of love, always love (with a capital L). Love of God, love for our fellow beings, love between man and woman. Ideal love, eternal love, love *in excelsior*. To her, earthly love was only to be found, or sought, between soul mates, that is, between two individuals destined for one another from all eternity. Extravagant? Unquestionably. Rare? Exceedingly. But what a treat for a hungry soul! What relief, after the sickening psychological and sociological dramas presented to us as slices of reality! In addition to being a writer she had unquestionable musical talent:

she sang, played with the harp, and was an accomplished pianist who gave concerts in which she improvised only. (A gift, this, which I have always secretly envied.)

Another woman writer whom I rediscovered during my Paris days was Lady Murasaki (*The Tale of Genji*). I must have been about twenty when I first read her. How I first came upon her work I no longer remember, unless it was that I was then reading widely in the field of Oriental literature, religion and philosophy more particularly. If Petronius Arbiter may be called the first novelist, what shall we call Lady Murasaki whose modern spirit expressed itself at a time when the great cathedrals of Europe and the first university had just begun to be built. Her 12th century Japan stands out in marked contrast to the subsequent periods of Japanese culture, much as do the glorious days of the Middle Ages in contrast to the Renaissance period in European history. In the midst of primitive conditions we have courtly manners, the practice of the arts, and frankness in intercourse. By comparison the Japan of today seems almost psychotic.

Shortly after my marriage I fell again upon Pierre Loti's *Madame Chrysanthème* (O Kikou San). Though this was, I believe, the first European book about Japan, I doubt very much that it is familiar to the Japanese reader of today. What a fantastic picture of Japan (region of Nagasaki) this book presents! Written with venom, spite and malice, it tickles the Westerner by its caricatural humor, by its gross distortion and pettiness of spirit. It is the exact opposite in spirit of his *Disenchanted*, a novel about Turkish life in a harem. This latter work is one I have read several times, always with the same sentimental fervor. Such wonderful, cultured women, accomplished in the arts, skilled in the art of seduction also, and ever veiled in mystery.

I cannot omit in passing the mention of Japanese fairy tales, which I came across when researching the fairy tales of other countries. Seeing the film *Kwaidan*, I recalled my reading of Lafcadio Hearn (fifty years ago), and of the striking impression which the Japanese fairy tales made upon me then. In many of the Japanese films I have seen in recent years I am reminded not only of the beauty and the imagination—shall I say the "echoes" of the Japanese soul—which they reveal, but also of the horror and the cruelty which seemingly also invests the Japanese psyche. The psychoanalysts have exposed for us the underlying sadism, the wanton cruelty, in our own Western fairy tales, Grimm's especially, which may possibly explain our infantile behavior as adults. But in the Japanese films and fairy tales there seems to be an exaggerated element of cruelty, just as there is another kind of exaggeration in Japanese erotic art. Perhaps I too am exaggerating in placing such emphasis on *Japanese* cruelty.

It may be supposed that I do a great deal of rereading. Such is not the case. It is only in late years I have taken to rereading old favorites. There are two books I must make mention of because they are the ones I have reread the most: Herman Hesse's *Siddhartha* (the last few pages especially), and Knut Hamsun's *Mysteries*. Of all the novels I have read, and God knows I have read scores of them, and despite the fact that I consider Dostoievski's novels the greatest of all, *Mysteries* nevertheless remains my favorite. I have never been able to discover if it was translated into Japanese. If not, as I suspect, may I close by recommending it to some enterprising Japanese publisher.

Henry Miller

/\.\/\.\/\.\/\.\

June 19th 1969

Dear Hoki-San—

Got your letter from London yesterday only. Wonder if you got telephone call from Joe Strick in Paris about possibility of small part in the "Cancer" film? I wrote you about this in one of my letters to London (c/o my British publisher) did you call for mail there?

I'm surprised you liked the look of London first sight. I have always thought of it as grim, monotonous, ugly. The people in the street are good, yes, very civil and helpful. I'll be there the 26th until the 30th—at the Savoy Hotel (A suite with Gerald! *de luxe*), one of the best hotels.

By now, you must be in Paris—and I hope got my letter (at Oko's) about George Belmont. Maybe you are already working for Strick?

I'll most likely stay at Hotel le Royal—212 Blvd. Raspail. I am telling them *not* to put any telephone calls thru for me, but turn them over to Gerald or to Paramount's secretary. So ask for Gerald if you phone me there. My room, a single, will have *one* big bed, so you will probably not want to stay there.

As it nears time to leave things get more and more hectic. Now I'm on roller skates! I look good and feel good. Hope it lasts. Don't know what I have to do in Paris precisely, nor for how long. So don't count too much on my going to St. Tropez or wherever. *If* I could get away from the job middle of August I would prefer to come home, rest a month, then go to Japan. We will see.

Bradley Smith told me the other day that about (2) years ago, on his way to Japan, he was seated on the plane next to a Japanese girl, who said she had been playing and singing at Imperial Gardens. She was very drunk and sick (because she had been given a big party night before leaving—ha ha!) He helped her and then gave her his phone at Ekura Hotel. She called next day and he said they spent 4 pleasant days. At this point we were interrupted and I never found out who the girl was. Could it have been Hoki Tokuda?

Nothing else new here. Is Puko still with you? Jeff is definitely in Japan. Connie talked to his father—said he was sending Jeff money there. Strange what? But I think it is only for a brief visit. (Maybe he met a Japanese girl in Paris?) Have a good time—I'm sure you are!

Yours
Henry-San

(From Henry in Paris to Hoki back home in California.)

DISILLUSION

/\/\/\/\/\/\

Dear Hoki-San—

I got your nice letter some days ago but no chance to reply until now. Always busy. Last 2 days in bed, because of bad food.

In a few minutes I go on TV at George's home for two hours. Did a two hour radio interview the other day. They are going to make a record of it and a small book—all in French. Tomorrow I see Marcel Marceau again about the film.

When I get home I will have lots of work to do—especially on Bradley's ("Bloody") book, as well as two others.

I doubt very much I will go to Tokyo. Am already tired out, disgusted with travel, and only too happy to be back home and enjoy life in my own sweet way. I have seen and talked to so many people that I don't want to see any one but a few close friends.

Tony is doing very well as a photographer and getting little jobs now and then. Today is his birthday and we will give him a birthday dinner in a nice restaurant—Oko is coming too—for dinner. First time I see her since you left.

Shushuen is having wonderful success with her film. All critics praise her highly. She sold it to Canada and some other country. Columbia B.C. wants to buy it—at a very good price!—but she wants more. Anyway, they want to do her next picture in Cambodia. She is trying to get Gerald (and Tony if possible) to go with her.

I enclose a few pages I wrote about a Japanese film we saw recently. Wrote it in bed at 3oc in the morning. Just found out that Michino sex means "anonymous sex"—that is, sex with any and everybody—sort of. Is that correct?

I hope you won't chase Harry and Connie away until I come back. I am very eager to get in pool and to play ping pong. This life here is very tiring and very monotonous. I will miss Tony, that's all. And maybe I will go back to see him sometime in winter (?) We got to know each other very well.

So, I will see you soon. And I won't mind if you are a little heavier. You look good at any weight. Give my best to Puko. I hope Arthur is good to her! A good hug for you.

Lots of love.

Henry-San

(Toward the end of September, Hoki returns to Japan to make a movie.)

.V.V.V.V.V.V.

Sept. 24th 1969

Chere petite Hoki-San—

You have hardly left and we all miss you already. "We" includes me, your loving husband. Especially *me*! How are you? How did Tokyo look to you on landing? Now you are once again in "the land of the sky blue waters". Banzai!

I haven't had letter from Mr. Tumata yet, but probably will in a day or two. I hope he is crediting me with a good sum. (But don't try to spend it all at once!)

I am still reading that book about Japanese language and customs. Very, very interesting. I see now why Japanese like to get drunk and why they are always forgiven for bad behavior when drunk. (*Very* interesting!)

It is a gray, bleak, dismal day here today. One of those days when you could commit suicide with pleasure. Instead I will take Michiyo to dinner and see "The Midnight Cowboy." (Ha ha!) Is it playing in Tokyo, I wonder?

Give warm greetings to your father-San and his wife. I suppose I shall see Keiko before I see Nikko. And Tomoko before Rokoko (whatever that means.)

DISILLUSION

When you are interviewed by newspaper or radio or whatever say that Henry-San (old-time "sukebei")* still loves his Hoki-San, still believes in her as much as ever, and only thinks of how to make her happy. O.K.?

Write me only when you feel like it. But I hope you feel like it now and then.

Love—
Henry

* "Sex maniac."

/\./\./\./\./\./\.\

Oct. 27th 1969

Dear Hoki-San—

"A Black Day at Black Rock"—yet who can say, what's good or bad for us? As I said in my card, Michiyo read your long letter to me the other day. The night before, she translated that article about us in the Woman's Magazine. And today comes another article from a Japanese magazine with a photo of you cutting the wedding cake, and another photo, presumably of you sitting with a girl at a table. (not translated yet, but am steeling myself for the bad news.)

Some day this week I am going up to Big Sur with Bob Snyder and do some film work there. I also have to visit my sister in the Rest Home near Monterey, as she is now slowly dying of cancer and is begging to see me.

This morning I got a letter from Tony telling me I have illusions about who my friends are—in Paris. If he only knew—that I have no illusions either about my friends nor my wives nor my idols. Right now I am living in that cold, clear light of truth which makes

159

everything equal—treachery, infidelity, cheating, lying, stealing, black-mailing or double dealing. It's all one, because people are what they are, and nobody can change them, not even God Almighty. We have to take what is handed out to us, like it or not. We have to read between the lines, whether the characters are Chinese or Japanese, whether legible or illegible, whether fact or fiction. I am writing you in English today, because my Japanese is not adequate.

Yesterday I opened your envelope (with returned cheques) from the bank, thinking it was mine. Very sorry. As of Sept 24th you had a balance of $709.69—from Security First Bank.

Now that you are not sure whether you are returning or not, what shall I do about the car? Turn it in? Or give it to the Salvation Army? It's in the name of *Mr.* Hiroka Miller, who does not exist, so what's the difference?

There are a thousand things I would like to tell you, but today is not the day for it. I am too lucid and the blade of my Samurai sword is so fine that even my warm breath on it would dull the edge.

Yesterday at ping pong (Kapers) some one handed me this quotation from Goethe: "Treat people as if they were what they ought to be and you will help them become what they are capable of becoming."

I wonder. I have been trying that for years but without great results. I think maybe it's better to just take people as they are and love them for what they are now. Thata way you have nothing to lose—or gain. You walk the tightrope, but there's always a net to protect you if you fall.

To change the dishwater . . . I certainly don't think it's a good idea for you to open a dress shop or any other kind of shop. I doubted the wisdom of it from the beginning but now I'm convinced of it. So, don't count on me to help you out, should you decide to come back. Nor would I suggest you bring your sister to live with us. Too many people have now seen the way we live— apart, that is—and I don't want to lose any more face. What we have to face, you and I, is whether we are going to continue living apart or begin living together. Thus far you have had everything your own way. And when things don't go your way you fall apart, go into a tizzy, threaten to have a nervous breakdown. It means you are behaving like a child. And you can't go on behaving like a child forever. Some day you must grow up.

I understand exactly what happened when Puko took up with Arthur. You must realize now how you lied to yourself about your own relationship with Puko. You needed her even more than she needed you. She was your puppet, the doll you never played with when you were a child. You put her above your own husband. He wanted you, he needed you, he loved you—but your little doll, your slave, came first. I remember so well your disgraceful behavior when we got married a second time. It was even worse than the first time. I hope to God I never tell any one of the shame you put me to. Nor the deep humiliation, as a man, that I suffered when after our big quarrel you begged me never to have any sex life with you!

More . . . I wonder if you have forgotten how before we decided to marry—when you were wondering desperately who would take you—I suggested that you marry the Chinese boy at the restaurant (Grand Star), I said—"You can marry him, but you don't have to sleep with him." And you replied—"Oh no, I would never do that. I would have to sleep with him." In other words you were ready to do for him what you would not do for me.

I have the memory of an elephant. I could tell you a hundred more similar stories—and you would answer—"but you misunderstood me!"

Hoki-San the only person you have ever fooled is yourself. How many times, when you have stood in front of me, and given me bare-faced lies, I thought to myself—"If only she could see herself in the mirror now, she would realize that no one could possibly believe her. It shows in her face, in every gesture she makes."

And in your letter to Michiyo you made a slip which was terribly revealing. You said you wished you could run into someone whom you could fall in love with—or words to that effect. And Michiyo, blushing and embarrassed, reads that to me. Jesus! What more can you do to hurt me?

Michiyo just translated the article in other Woman's Magazine. Now I am hurt even more. Now you tell the whole world there is no sex business—I am just like your grandfather! (ouch!) And all that stuff about the hippies and the Jaguar. God, it makes me sick. What drivel! What trivia! And how immature it all is! And the diamonds and emeralds! What shit! How I detest all that!

And what a lie to talk about our "companionship," our "talks." If only we had real talks! If only there were some companionship! What are you doing—lying to yourself and the world? When are you going to talk reality, truth?

I have spoken of the terrible things you've said and done. I also remember some beautiful moments—so few, so far between. Maybe only a half-dozen in all, in all the time I know you. Think of it! Balzac once wrote that he could remember only three or four happy days in all his life. And I who love you can say the same.

When I put on your recording (Sony) I melt. Yes, I go to pieces, just hearing your voice. It was your voice and your eyes that got me. And still does. And for that I forget all the misery you cause me. What a fool! What a romantic! "A romantchu." Everything has been just like a *"musei"*—wet dream.

But I must cure myself. I can't go on this way. It kills me.

I am not your "grandfather". I don't want Platonic love, I have nothing to do with hippies. I do not want companionship alone. And what companionship have we really had? You have treated me worse than you would an enemy. You have humiliated me before your friends and before the whole world. *Me!* Me, who was your one refuge, who married you even though he knew you didn't love me. If I was a truly great soul I would have expected nothing of you. But I am not that great. I am human. I expect something of you. And if you can't give it to me I think we should separate. Why live out a lie? You say you didn't marry for economic reasons. Maybe you didn't. But *why did you marry*? I remember how in Stefanino's, when I said I would marry you, I remember how you said you would make me a good wife. But have you? Can you honestly say yes? Think about it. Ask yourself if you have been

honest and fair with me. I can't help loving you. It's like a disease.
But I won't go on living with you unless you can show some love
and affection. I'd rather kill myself than go on living this way
forever.

Your
Henry-San

EDITOR'S NOTE: *Instead of staying in Japan, Hoki did return to
Henry in December 1969. The stresses and strains of the relationship continued until May of 1970, when they finally separated. Hoki
moved to Marina del Rey and opened her boutique shop in Beverly
Hills. She continued to visit Henry and he wrote to her spasmodi-
cally until 1975.*